# Newnes Electronics Toolkit

# Newnes Electronics Toolkit

Geoff Phillips

Newnes
An imprint of Butterworth-Heinemann Ltd
Linacre House, Jordan Hill, Oxford OX2 8DP

ℛ   A member of the Reed Elsevier plc group

OXFORD LONDON BOSTON
MUNICH NEW DELHI SINGAPORE SYDNEY
TOKYO TORONTO WELLINGTON

First published 1993
Reprinted 1994, 1995

© Geoff Phillips 1993

**British Library Cataloguing in Publication Data**
A catalogue record for this book is available from
the British Library

**Library of Congress Cataloguing in Publication Data**
A catalogue record for this book is available from
the Library of Congress

ISBN 0 7506 0929 X

Printed in England by Clays Ltd, St Ives plc

# Contents

# Preface

Electronics engineers involved in the design and development of electronic circuits are constantly referring to technical data. The speed and efficiency of the design and development process is usually hampered by the problem of locating the data quickly and then assimilating it. The objective of this book was to bring together fundamental facts, concepts and applications of electronic components and circuits and present them in a clear, concise, and unambiguous format, resulting in a reference book that the engineer would rather have on his desk alongside his calculator or on his bench alongside his oscilloscope, rather than on the bookshelf. The engineer's job is not finished when the circuit diagram has been completed, the design for manufacture process is just as important if volume production is to be undertaken. The task of component selection and second or even third sourcing of alternative components is an essential part of the design process. This book attempts to assist the engineer with the component sourcing process by the inclusion of tables which present the electrical and mechanical parameters of electronic components which have evolved to be "industry standard" devices. The tables are in a format where the parameters of components from different manufacturers may be compared easily and a decision made as to their suitability for the engineer's circuit.

The presentation and layout of the data, circuit diagrams, and text in this book was achieved by the use of the state-of-the-art computer applications. The text, tables and drawings were prepared by the author using Word for Windows by Microsoft. The circuit diagrams and component symbols were prepared by the author using an application called ISIS Illustrator by Labcenter Electronics.

# 1 Resistors

When a voltage is applied to a pure resistance, current flows in direct proportion to the voltage irrespective of how it may be varying.

The current through a resistor at any instant in time may be shown as:

$$i = \frac{v}{R}$$

v = the applied voltage at the same instant in time
R = the resistor's resistance in ohms

THE CURRENT THROUGH THE RESISTOR FOLLOWS
THE VOLTAGE IRRESPECTIVE OF HOW IT MAY BE CHANGING

## Power in a resistor

$$= i^2 R$$  or  $$= \frac{v^2}{R}$$  **WATTS**

Where i and v are r.m.s. or dc values of current and voltage respectively.

 **Rules of thumb**

- When current is driven through a resistor, the input lead becomes positive.
- The total resistance of two resistors in parallel is product over sum (R1 x R2) / (R1 + R2).
- When analysing a complex circuit, ignore a resistor which is in parallel and > 10x.

## Design pitfalls

### Over-voltage
Always check that the resistor will not be subjected to a transient voltage which exceeds the manufacturer's maximum rating. An endurance test of the prototype may not reveal a problem but production units could fail.

### Over-dissipation
If a 6W resistor is run at 6W or even 5W its surface temperature may be high enough to scorch printed circuit boards, damage surrounding components, or even melt solder. Always refer to the manufacturer's data sheet regarding surface temperature versus watts.

### Pulsed power
Ensure that the resistor is capable of withstanding transient current surges.

# Uses of a resistor
## To derive a current from a voltage

An LED cannot be connected directly to a dc supply as it is a low impedance and the current would be too high. A resistor may be used to give a current proportional to the applied voltage and in the example shown the resistor sets the current to approximately 10mA.

## To derive a voltage from a current

R1 derives a current of 0.1mA from the 10V supply to drive the base of TR1. TR1 has a gain of 100 and so 10mA flows in the collector. The collector of a transistor is a constant current source and the circuit would operate with R2 replaced by a short circuit. If an output voltage is required from the circuit however R2 is used to derive a voltage proportional to TR1's collector current.

## Pull down

When the switch SW1 is opened, the base current to TR1 is interrupted and the transistor should switch off. There is leakage current across the collector-base junction however which flows back into the base and may cause the transistor to continue to conduct. Resistor R3 gives a pull-down effect to the base providing a path for the leakage current and assisting the turn-off of the transistor. R3 also improves the speed of turn-off in switching circuits.

## Timing, filtering
See uses of a capacitor.

## Potential division

Two resistors in series constitute a potential divider which gives a voltage Vout equal to R2/(R1 + R2) times the input voltage.

$$\text{Vout} = \text{Vin}\ \frac{R2}{R1 + R2}$$

# Resistor colour codes
### E12 and E24 series (4 band)

| COLOUR | 1st & 2nd DIGITS | MULTIPLIER | TOLERANCE |
|--------|------------------|------------|-----------|
| BLACK | 0 | 1 | - |
| BROWN | 1 | 10 | ±1% |
| RED | 2 | $10^2$ | ±2% |
| ORANGE | 3 | $10^3$ | - |
| YELLOW | 4 | $10^4$ | - |
| GREEN | 5 | $10^5$ | - |
| BLUE | 6 | $10^6$ | - |
| VIOLET | 7 | $10^7$ | - |
| GREY | 8 | $10^8$ | - |
| WHITE | 9 | $10^9$ | - |
| GOLD | - | $10^{-1}$ | ±5% |
| SILVER | - | $10^{-2}$ | ±10% |

*Examples*

| COLOUR | VALUE | WRITTEN AS (BS1852) |
|--------|-------|---------------------|
| RED-RED-SILVER | 0.22 ohms | R22 |
| BROWN-BLACK-GOLD | 1 ohm | 1R0 |
| BROWN-BLACK-BLACK | 10 ohms | 10R |
| BROWN-RED-BROWN | 120 ohms | 120R |
| BLUE-GREY-RED | 6.8 kilohms | 6K8 |
| GREEN-BLUE-ORANGE | 56 kilohms | 56K |
| BROWN-RED-YELLOW | 120 kilohms | 120K |
| GREY-RED-GREEN | 8.2 Megohms | 8M2 |

**E48 and E96 series (5 band)**

| COLOUR | 1st & 2nd & 3rd DIGITS | MULTIPLIER | TOLERANCE |
|--------|:----:|:----:|:----:|
| BLACK | 0 | 1 | - |
| BROWN | 1 | 10 | ±1% |
| RED | 2 | $10^2$ | ±2% |
| ORANGE | 3 | $10^3$ | - |
| YELLOW | 4 | $10^4$ | - |
| GREEN | 5 | $10^5$ | - |
| BLUE | 6 | $10^6$ | - |
| VIOLET | 7 | $10^7$ | - |
| GREY | 8 | $10^8$ | - |
| WHITE | 9 | $10^9$ | - |
| GOLD | - | $10^{-1}$ | ±5% |
| SILVER | - | $10^{-2}$ | ±10% |

*Examples*

| COLOUR | VALUE | WRITTEN AS (BS1852) |
|--------|:----:|:----:|
| RED-BROWN-GREEN-SILVER | 2.15 ohms | 2R15 |
| ORANGE-ORANGE-RED-GOLD | 33.2 ohm | 33R2 |
| GREEN-WHITE-BLACK-BLACK | 590 ohms | 590R |
| BROWN-RED-BROWN-BROWN | 1.21 kilohms | 1K21 |
| ORANGE-ORANGE-RED-RED | 33.2 kilohms | 33K2 |
| BROWN-RED-VIOLET-ORANGE | 127 kilohms | 127K |
| VIOLET-GREY-VIOLET-YELLOW | 7.87 Megohms | 7M87 |
| RED-RED-BLUE-GREEN | 22.6 Megohms | 22M6 |

The BS1852 style of writing the resistor value avoids errors caused by the decimal point failing to reproduce clearly on drawings and photocopies. The letter R is used to signify ohms as the Greek letter Ω is not usually available on computer printers.

# Passive component code letters

## Tolerance code letters

The tolerance of resistors and capacitors is often denoted by a code letter which should not be confused with decimal prefixes of the component's value. For example a capacitor marked with 10K is a 10 uF capacitor having a tolerance of 10%.

| CODE LETTER | TOLERANCE |
|:---:|:---:|
| A | ±0.05% |
| B | ±0.1% |
| C | ±0.25% |
| D | ±0.5% |
| F | ±1% |
| G | ±2% |
| J | ±5% |
| K | ±10% |
| M | ±20% |
| N | ±30% |
| Q | -10%, +30% |
| T | -10%, +50% |
| S | -20%, +50% |
| Z | -20%, +80% |

## Temperature Coefficient Code Letters

Less common is a letter code to signify the component's drift in value with temperature.

| CODE LETTER | TEMP COEFF |
|:---:|:---:|
| Y | 15 ppm / °C |
| D | 25 ppm / °C |
| C | 50 ppm / °C |
| Z | 100 ppm / °C |
| G | 150 ppm / °C |
| X | 250 ppm / °C |

# Derivation of E- resistor values

### E12 Values

In the circuit below, the current flowing is 10A. Suppose we wish to reduce the current in equal steps. If resistor values of 2, 3, 4, 5, 6 7, 8, 9, 10 ohms were chosen as standard values then the current would reduce in unequal steps.

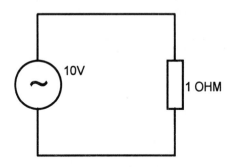

| RESISTANCE | CURRENT |
|:---:|:---:|
| 1 ohm | 10.0A |
| 2 ohm | 5.00A |
| 3 ohm | 3.33A |
| 4 ohm | 2.50A |
| 5 ohm | 2.00A |
| 6 ohm | 1.67A |
| 7 ohm | 1.43A |
| 8 ohm | 1.25A |
| 9 ohm | 1.11A |
| 10 ohm | 1.00A |

In the early days of resistor manufacture, tolerances of 10% were achievable. If a resistor of standard value 1 ohm was chosen then during manufacture the highest value allowable. would be 1.1 ohm. It is reasonable to make the next highest standard value 20% higher on the reasoning that when it was at its minimum tolerance, then its value would overlap with 1.1 ohm ( 1.2 ohm x 0.9 = 1.08 ohm).

The 12th root of 10 is 1.2115 and this a convenient number of increments. If the standard values of resistors are set at 12 increments of x1.2115, then equal steps of reduction in current in the circuit above may be achieved.

| EQUAL STEPS OF 12th ROOT OF 10 | E12 VALUES ACTUALLY CHOSEN | CURRENT IN CIRCUIT | % REDUCTION IN CURRENT EACH STEP |
|:---:|:---:|:---:|:---:|
| 1.0000 | 1 | 10.00 | |
| 1.2115 | 1.2 | 8.33 | 16.67 |
| 1.4678 | 1.5 | 6.67 | 20.00 |
| 1.7783 | 1.8 | 5.56 | 16.67 |
| 2.1544 | 2.2 | 4.55 | 18.18 |
| 2.6102 | 2.7 | 3.70 | 18.52 |
| 3.1623 | 3.3 | 3.03 | 18.18 |
| 3.8312 | 3.9 | 2.56 | 15.38 |
| 4.6416 | 4.7 | 2.13 | 17.02 |
| 5.6234 | 5.6 | 1.79 | 16.07 |
| 6.8129 | 6.8 | 1.47 | 17.65 |
| 8.2540 | 8.2 | 1.22 | 17.07 |
| 10.0000 | 10 | 1.00 | 18.00 |

The reader is left to decide why 2.7 was chosen instead of 2.6, 3.3 instead of 3.2 and 3.9 instead of 3.8. A similar anomaly exists in the choice of the preferred resistor values in the E24 range shown on the next page. For the E48 and E96 ranges however, the preferred values have been chosen as steps of the 48th and 96th root of 10, rounded to one decimal place.

## E24 resistor values

| 24 EQUAL STEPS OF 24th ROOT OF 10 | ACTUAL E24 VALUES CHOSEN |
|---|---|
| 10.0000 | 10 |
| 11.0069 | 11 |
| 12.1153 | 12 |
| 13.3352 | 13 |
| 14.6780 | 15 |
| 16.1560 | 16 |
| 17.7828 | 18 |
| 19.5734 | 20 |
| 21.5444 | 22 |
| 23.7137 | 24 |
| 26.1016 | 27 |
| 28.7299 | 30 |
| 31.6228 | 33 |
| 34.8070 | 36 |
| 38.3119 | 39 |
| 42.1697 | 43 |
| 46.4159 | 47 |
| 51.0897 | 51 |
| 56.2342 | 56 |
| 61.8966 | 62 |
| 68.1292 | 68 |
| 74.9895 | 75 |
| 82.5405 | 82 |
| 90.8518 | 91 |
| 100.0000 | 100 |

## E48 resistor values

| 48 EQUAL STEPS OF 48th ROOT OF 10 | ACTUAL E48 VALUES CHOSEN |
|---|---|
| 10 | 10 |
| 10.4914 | 10.5 |
| 11.0069 | 11.0 |
| 11.5478 | 11.5 |
| 12.1153 | 12.1 |
| 12.7106 | 12.7 |
| 13.3352 | 13.3 |
| 13.9905 | 14.0 |
| 14.6780 | 14.7 |
| 15.3993 | 15.4 |
| 16.1560 | 16.2 |
| 16.9499 | 16.9 |
| 17.7828 | 17.8 |
| 18.6566 | 18.7 |
| 19.5734 | 19.6 |
| 20.5352 | 20.5 |
| 21.5443 | 21.5 |
| 22.6030 | 22.6 |
| 23.7137 | 23.7 |
| 24.8790 | 24.9 |
| 26.1016 | 26.1 |
| 27.3842 | 27.4 |
| 28.7298 | 28.7 |
| 30.1416 | 30.1 |
| 31.6228 | 31.6 |
| 33.1767 | 33.2 |
| 34.8070 | 34.8 |
| 36.5174 | 36.5 |
| 38.3118 | 38.3 |
| 40.1945 | 40.2 |
| 42.1696 | 42.2 |
| 44.2418 | 44.2 |
| 46.4158 | 46.4 |
| 48.6967 | 48.7 |
| 51.0896 | 51.1 |
| 53.6002 | 53.6 |
| 56.2341 | 56.2 |
| 58.9974 | 59.0 |
| 61.8965 | 61.9 |
| 64.9381 | 64.9 |
| 68.1291 | 68.1 |
| 71.4770 | 71.5 |
| 74.9893 | 75.0 |
| 78.6743 | 78.7 |
| 82.5403 | 82.5 |
| 86.5963 | 86.6 |
| 90.8516 | 90.9 |
| 95.3161 | 95.3 |
| 100 | 100 |

## E96 resistor values

| 96 STEPS OF 96th ROOT OF 10 | E96 VALUES CHOSEN | 96 STEPS OF 96th ROOT OF 10 | E96 VALUES CHOSEN |
|---|---|---|---|
| 10.0000 | 10.0 | 32.3904 | 32.4 |
| 10.2428 | 10.2 | 33.1767 | 33.2 |
| 10.4914 | 10.5 | 33.9820 | 34.0 |
| 10.7461 | 10.7 | 34.8070 | 34.8 |
| 11.0069 | 11.0 | 35.6519 | 35.7 |
| 11.2741 | 11.3 | 36.5174 | 36.5 |
| 11.5478 | 11.5 | 37.4038 | 37.4 |
| 11.8281 | 11.8 | 38.3118 | 38.3 |
| 12.1153 | 12.1 | 39.2419 | 39.2 |
| 12.4094 | 12.4 | 40.1945 | 40.2 |
| 12.7106 | 12.7 | 41.1702 | 41.2 |
| 13.0192 | 13.0 | 42.1696 | 42.2 |
| 13.3352 | 13.3 | 43.1933 | 43.2 |
| 13.6589 | 13.7 | 44.2418 | 44.2 |
| 13.9905 | 14.0 | 45.3158 | 45.3 |
| 14.3301 | 14.3 | 46.4158 | 46.4 |
| 14.6780 | 14.7 | 47.5426 | 47.5 |
| 15.0343 | 15.0 | 48.6967 | 48.7 |
| 15.3993 | 15.4 | 49.8788 | 49.9 |
| 15.7731 | 15.8 | 51.0896 | 51.1 |
| 16.1560 | 16.2 | 52.3298 | 52.3 |
| 16.5482 | 16.5 | 53.6002 | 53.6 |
| 16.9499 | 16.9 | 54.9013 | 54.9 |
| 17.3613 | 17.4 | 56.2340 | 56.2 |
| 17.7828 | 17.8 | 57.5991 | 57.6 |
| 18.2145 | 18.2 | 58.9974 | 59.0 |
| 18.6566 | 18.7 | 60.4295 | 60.4 |
| 19.1095 | 19.1 | 61.8965 | 61.9 |
| 19.5734 | 19.6 | 63.3990 | 63.4 |
| 20.0486 | 20.0 | 64.9381 | 64.9 |
| 20.5352 | 20.5 | 66.5144 | 66.5 |
| 21.0337 | 21.0 | 68.1291 | 68.1 |
| 21.5443 | 21.5 | 69.7829 | 69.8 |
| 22.0673 | 22.1 | 71.4769 | 71.5 |
| 22.6030 | 22.6 | 73.2121 | 73.2 |
| 23.1517 | 23.2 | 74.9893 | 75.0 |
| 23.7137 | 23.7 | 76.8097 | 76.8 |
| 24.2894 | 24.3 | 78.6742 | 78.7 |
| 24.8790 | 24.9 | 80.5841 | 80.6 |
| 25.4829 | 25.5 | 82.5403 | 82.5 |
| 26.1016 | 26.1 | 84.5439 | 84.5 |
| 26.7352 | 26.7 | 86.5963 | 86.6 |
| 27.3842 | 27.4 | 88.6984 | 88.7 |
| 28.0489 | 28.0 | 90.8516 | 90.9 |
| 28.7298 | 28.7 | 93.0570 | 93.1 |
| 29.4272 | 29.4 | 95.3160 | 95.3 |
| 30.1416 | 30.1 | 97.6298 | 97.6 |
| 30.8733 | 30.9 | 100.0000 | 100.0 |
| 31.6227 | 31.6 | | |

# Resistor selection chart

| | COMPOSITION | FILM | | | | WIREWOUND | | | SMD |
|---|---|---|---|---|---|---|---|---|---|
| **TYPE** | | | | | | | | | |
| **GENERAL ATTRIBUTES** | Low inductance | Accurate tolerances available. Low drift and good temperature coefficient. | | | | Higher power and pulsed power than film type. | | | Lower wattage Low inductance |
| **RESISTOR TYPE** | CARBON COMPOSITION | CARBON FILM | METAL FILM | METAL OXIDE | METAL GLAZE | ALUMINIUM CLAD | VITREOUS ENAMEL | CEMENTED | SMD CHIP |
| **CON-STRUCTION** | Moulded carbon | Homogeneous carbon film on ceramic body into which a helical groove is cut | Homogeneous metal alloy film on ceramic body into which a helical groove is cut | Homogeneous tin-oxide film on glass body into which a helical groove is cut | Metal-glazed film on a ceramic body | Wirewound housed in an aluminium case | Resistance wire is wound on a ceramic rod and coated with a vitreous enamel | Resistance wire is wound on a ceramic rod and coated with a silicon cement | Resistive paste applied to a ceramic monolith. Laser-cut trimmed to value |
| **ADVANTAGES** | Low inductance Good pulse handling Fair high voltage peformance | Low cost/performance ratio | High accuracy available. Low temp drift | Good temperature coefficient, very low noise | High values High voltage | High power dissipation. May be heat-sunk | High pulsed power capability | High pulsed power capability | Small physical size |
| **DIS-ADVANTAGES** | Poor tolerance Poor long term drift Poor temp coef High noise Poor availability | Modest temp drift | Higher cost | Higher cost | Limited value range | Higher inductance than film | Higher cost | Higher inductance than film | Limited wattage and voltage ratings |
| **RESISTANCE RANGE AVAILABLE** | 10R to 22M | 1R to 10M | 5R to 10M | 0R2 to 100k | 100k to 22M | 0R01 to 120k | 0R1 to 100k | 0R1 to 33k | 1R to 10M |
| **WATTAGES AVAILABLE** | 0.25W to 1W | 0.125W to 2W | 0.25W to 3W | 0.5W TO 7W | 0.25W to 1W | 10W to 50W | 2.5W to 12W | 3W to 20W | 0.25W (1206 style) |
| **TEMPERATURE COEFFICIENT** | +200 to -2000 ppm/°C | +200 to -1000 ppm/°C | ±50 ppm/°C | ±200 ppm/°C | ±200 ppm/°C | ±100 ppm/°C | +200 max ppm/°C | ±100 ppm/°C | ±200 ppm/°C |
| **MANUFAC-TURERS** | VTM Series BT Neohm CBT 1/2 | Neohm CFR VTM DC Philips CR Piher PR | Philips MRS Neohm LR Welwyn GMF, MFR | Neohm ROX | Philips VR VTM GH | Arcol HS Welwyn WH | Welwyn W | ERG 74ER Philips AC03 - 20 | Philips RC VTM RGC |

# 1/4W carbon film resistors

| MANFR | TYPE No | WATTAGE | DERATING | RANGE | TOL | TEMP COEF | MAX V | MAX TEMP | MAX DIMENSIONS |
|---|---|---|---|---|---|---|---|---|---|
| NEOHM | CFR25 | 0.33w @ 70°C | Linearly to 155°C | 1R to 10M E24 | ±5% | +200 to -800 ppm / °C | 250V rms | | 2.5 / 6.7 / 0.6 |
| PHILIPS | CR25 | 0.33w @ 70°C | Linearly to 125°C | 1R to 10M E24 | ±2%,±5% | -200 to -600 ppm / °C | 250V rms | | 2.5 / 6.5 / 0.6 |
| PIHER | PR025 | 0.25w @ 70°C | Linearly to 155°C | 1R to 10M | ±2%,±5% | -150 to -800 ppm / °C | 250V rms | +155°C | 2.6 / 7.0 / 0.6 |
| ROHM | R25X | 0.33w @ 70°C | Linearly to 155°C | 10R to 3M3 | ±2%,±5% | +300 to -1000 ppm / °C | 300V rms | +155°C | 2.5 / 6.6 / 0.63 |
| VTM | DC105 | 0.25w @ 70°C | Linearly to 125°C | 1R to 10M E24 | ±5% | -200 to -900 ppm / °C | 250V rms | | 2.5 / 6.8 / 0.6 |
| WELWYN | GCF 1/4 | 0.25w @ 70°C | Linearly to x°C | 1R to 22M | ±5% | -x to -x ppm / °C | 250V rms | +155°C | 2.5 / 6.4 / 0.6 |

**1/2W carbon film resistors**

| MANFR | TYPE No | WATTAGE | DERATING | RANGE | TOL | TEMP COEF | MAX V | MAX TEMP | MAX DIMENSIONS |
|---|---|---|---|---|---|---|---|---|---|
| DRALORIC | LCA0411 | 0.5W @ 70°C | Linearly to 155°C | 0R22 to 10M E24 | ±2%,±5% | -250 to -800 ppm / °C | 350V rms | 155°C | 3.7 / 10.5 / 0.7 |
| NEOHM | CFR50 | 0.66W @ 70°C | Linearly to 155°C | 1R to 10M E24 | ±5% | +200 to -850 ppm / °C | 350V rms |  | 4.0 / 9.9 / 0.7 |
| PIHER | PR05 | 0.5W @ 70°C | Linearly to 155°C | 1R to 10M | ±2%,±5% | -130 to -800 ppm / °C | 350V rms | 155°C | 3.7 / 9.5 / 0.6 |
| ROEDER-STEIN | SK4 | 0.6W @ 70°C | Linearly to 125°C | 1R to 30M | ±5% | -300 to -1200 ppm / °C | 500V rms | 155°C | 4.1 / 12 / 0.8 |
| WELWYN | GCF 1/2 | 0.5W @ 70°C | Linearly to 155°C | 1R to 2M2 | ±5% | -300 to -800 ppm / °C | 350V rms | 155°C | 3.7 / 9.0 / 0.7 |
| VTM | DC115 | 0.5W @ 70°C | Linearly to 125°C | 1R to 10M E24 | ±5% | -200 to -800 ppm / °C | 250V rms |  | 4.0 / 10 / 0.7 |

**1W carbon film resistors**

| MANFR | TYPE No | WATTAGE | DERATING | RANGE | TOL | TEMP COEF | MAX V | MAX TEMP | MAX DIMENSIONS |
|---|---|---|---|---|---|---|---|---|---|
| DRALORIC | LCA0719 | 1W @ 70°C | Linearly to 155°C | 2R2 to 20M E24 | ±2%,±5% | -250 to -700 ppm / °C | 750V rms | | 6.5  18.5  0.8 |
| NEOHM | CFR100 | 1W @ 70°C | Linearly to 155°C | 1R to 10M E24 | ±5% | +200 to -900 ppm / °C | 500V rms | | 5.0  14  0.8 |
| PIHER | PR01 | 1W @ 70°C | Linearly to 125°C | 1R to 10M | ±2%,±5% | -150 to -800 ppm / °C | 500V rms | | 5.0  13  0.8 |
| ROEDER-STEIN | SK5 | 1.1W @ 70°C | Linearly to 125°C | 1R to 24M E24 | ±5% | -200 to -1200 ppm / °C | 750V rms | 155°C | 6  16  0.8 |

**1/4W metal film resistors**

| MANFR | TYPE No | WATTAGE | DERATING | RANGE | TOL | TEMP COEF | MAX V | MAX TEMP | MAX DIMENSIONS |
|---|---|---|---|---|---|---|---|---|---|
| NEOHM | LR0204 | 0.25w @ 70°C | Linearly to 160°C | 10R to 470k E24 | ±1,2,5% | ±100 ppm / °C | 250V rms | 125°C | 1.8, 3.7, 0.45 |
| PHILIPS | MRS16T | 0.4W @ 70°C | Linearly to 155°C | 4R99 to 1M E24/E96 | ±1% | ±50 ppm / °C | 200V rms | 125°C | 1.9, 3.7, 0.5 |
| PIHER | PM25 | 0.25W @ 70°C | Linearly to 150°C | 10R to 1M | ±1% | ±50 ppm / °C | 250V rms | 155 °C | 2.3, 6.5, 0.6 |
| ROEDER-STEIN | MK1 | 0.4W @ 70°C | Linearly to 175°C | 0R22 to 5M1 | ±1,2,5% | ±50 ppm / °C | 250V rms | 170 °C | 1.6, 4.0, 0.5 |
| VTM | GP490 | 0.4W @ 70°C | Linearly to 155°C | 1R to 5M1 E96 | ±1% | ±50 ppm / °C | 200V rms | 155 °C | 1.6, 4.0, 0.52 |
| WELWYN | MFR3 | 0.4W @ 70°C | Linearly to 155°C | 1R to 1M E96 | ±1%,±2% | ±50 ppm / °C 10R to 150k | 200V rms | 155 °C | 1.8, 3.5, 0.5 |

**1/2W metal film resistors**

| MANFR | TYPE No | WATTAGE | DERATING | RANGE | TOL | TEMP COEF | MAX V | MAX TEMP | MAX DIMENSIONS |
|---|---|---|---|---|---|---|---|---|---|
| DRALORIC | SMA0204 | 0.5W @ 70°C | Linearly to 155°C | 1R to 10M E24/E96 | ±0.1,0.25, 0.5,1,2,5% | ±15,25,50, 100 ppm / °C | 200V rms | - | 1.8 / 3.6 / 0.5 |
| NEOHM | LR1 | 0.5W@ 70°C | Linearly to 155°C | 1R to 1M E24 | ±1%, 2% | ±100,±50 ppm / °C | 350V rms | 125°C | 2.5 / 6.7 / 0.6 |
| PHILIPS | MRS25 | 0.6W @ 70°C | Linearly to 155°C | 1R to 10M E24/E96 | ±1% | ±50 to ±100 ppm / °C | 350V rms | 125°C | 2.5 / 7.0 / 0.63 |
| VTM | GP491 | 0.6W @ 70°C | Linearly to 155°C | 1R to 10M E24/E96 | ±1% | ±50 ppm / °C | 350V rms | 155 °C | 2.5 / 6.0 / 0.62 |
| WELWYN | MFR4 | 0.5W @ 70°C | Linearly to 155°C | 1R to 1M | ±0.5%,±1%, ±2% | ±50 ppm / °C 10R to 150k | 350V rms | 155 °C | 2.3 / 6.2 / 0.6 |

1/2W metal oxide film resistors

| MANFR | TYPE No | WATTAGE | DERATING | RANGE | TOL | TEMP COEF | MAX V | MAX TEMP | MAX DIMENSIONS |
|---|---|---|---|---|---|---|---|---|---|
| DRALORIC | SXA0411 | 0.7W @ 70°C | Linearly to 210°C | 1R to 10M E24/E96 | ±1% | ±50 to ±100 ppm / °C | 350V rms | 125°C | 2.5, 7.0, 0.63 |
| NEOHM | ROX0410 | 0.5W @ 70°C | Linearly to 235°C | 0R2 to 100k E24 | ±2%, 5% | ±300 ppm / °C | 250V rms | 200°C | 3.5, 10, 0.7 |
| WELWYN | MO 1/2 S | 0.5W @ 70°C | Linearly to 235°C | 10R to 50k E24 | ±5%,±10% | ±350 ppm / °C | 250V rms | 155 °C | 2.3, 6.2, 0.6 |

**1/4W metal glaze resistors**

| MANFR | TYPE No | WATTAGE | DERATING | RANGE | TOL | TEMP COEF | MAX V | MAX TEMP | MAX DIMENSIONS |
|---|---|---|---|---|---|---|---|---|---|
| PHILIPS | VR25 | 0.25W@ 70°C | Linearly to 155°C | 100k - 10M E24,±5% | ±1%,E24/96 ±5%, E24 | ±200 ppm / °C | 1600V dc 1150V rms | 155°C | 2.5↓ ←7.5→ 0.6→ |
| VTM | GH82 | 0.25W@ 70°C | Linearly to 155°C | 100k to 22M E12,24,96 | ±1,5,10% | ±200 ppm / °C | 1600V dc 1150V rms | 155 °C | 2.5↓ ←6.0→ 0.62→ |

**1/2W metal glaze resistors**

| MANFR | TYPE No | WATTAGE | DERATING | RANGE | TOL | TEMP COEF | MAX V | MAX TEMP | MAX DIMENSIONS |
|-------|---------|---------|----------|-------|-----|-----------|-------|----------|----------------|
| PHILIPS | VR37 | 0.5w @ 70°C | Linearly to 155°C | 100k - 33M E24 | ±1%, E24/96 ±5%, E24 | ±200 ppm / °C | 3.5kV dc 2.5kV rms | 155°C | 3.7 / 10 / 0.7 |
| VTM | GH84 | 0.5w @ 70°C | Linearly to 155°C | 100k to 33M E24,96 | ±1%,5% | ±200 ppm / °C | 3.5kV dc 2.5kV rms | 155 °C | 4.0 / 9.0 / 0.7 |

**1W metal glaze resistors**

| MANFR | TYPE No | WATTAGE | DERATING | RANGE | TOL | TEMP COEF | MAX V | MAX TEMP | MAX DIMENSIONS |
|---|---|---|---|---|---|---|---|---|---|
| PHILIPS | VR68 | 1w @ 70°C | Linearly to 155°C | 100k - 68M E24,E96 | ±1%, E24/96 ±5%, E24 | ±200 ppm / °C | 10kV dc 7kV rms | 155°C | 6.8 / 19 / 0.8 |
| VTM | GH86 | 1w @ 70°C | Linearly to 155°C | 100k to 68M E24,96 | ±1%,5% | ±200 ppm / °C | 10kV dc 7kV rms | 155 °C | 6.8 / 16.5 / 0.7 |

7W ceramic case wire-wound resistors

| MANFR | TYPE No | WATTAGE | TEMP RISE AT 7W | RANGE | TOL | TEMP COEF | MAX V | MAX DIMENSIONS |
|---|---|---|---|---|---|---|---|---|
| ISKRA | EIZ1107 | 7W at 70°C | 230°C | 0R1 to 15k | ±5%, E24 ±10%,E12 | <0.56R +1300 other -80 to +400 ppm/°C | - | 6.5 / 6.5 / 38 / 0.82 |
| MEC MICRON | MS- | 7W at 70°C | 180°C | 0R51 to 56k | | | | 10.5 / 10 / 36.5 / 0.81 |
| NEOHM | RA7 | 7W at 70°C | 200°C | 0R1 to 6k8 | ±10%, ±5% | ±20 to +250 ppm/°C | Square root of 7 x R | 9.3 / 9.3 / 26 / 0.82 |
| VTM | KH 210-8/0 | 7W @ 70°C | 225°C | 0R11 to 33k | ±5%, E24 ±10%,E12 | -80 to +500 ppm/°C | Square root of 7 x R | 6.43 / 6.43 / 39 / 0.82 |

## 3W cement coated wire-wound resistors

| MANFR | TYPE No | WATTAGE | TEMP RISE AT 3W | RANGE | TOL | TEMP COEF | MAX V | MAX TEMP | MAX DIMENSIONS |
|---|---|---|---|---|---|---|---|---|---|
| PHILIPS | AC03 | 3W at 40°C | 275°C | 0R1 to 8R2 10R to 3k | 10%, 5%, E24 | -80 to +140 ppm / °C | 1000V dc | 350°C | 5.5 / 13 / 0.8 |
| ISKRA | EIZ1003 | 3W at 70°C | 275°C | 0R1 to 15k | ±5%, E24 ±10%, E12 | -80 to +1300 ppm / °C | - | 205°C | 5.0 / 34 / 0.82 |
| VTM | CR272-0 | 3.5W@ 70°C | 260°C | 0R1 to 15k E24 | ±5% | ±40 ppm / °C | Square-root of 3.5 x R V rms | 350 °C | 5.6 / 17 / 0.8 |
| WELWYN | WA84 | 2.5W @ 70°C | | 0R01 to2k2 | ±5,10% | >1R:200 <1R:350 ppm / °C | 100V rms | 275 °C | 5.2 / 14.5 / 0.8 |

# 2 Capacitors

 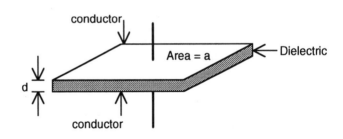

Electrical symbol            Parallel plate capacitor

## Definition

Capacitance is the property which exists when two conductors are brought in close proximity to each other and are then able to store electrical charge.

The capacitance is increased if the area of the conductors is increased or the distance between them is reduced. The insulating material between the conductors is called the dielectric and also affects the value of capacitance.

### Capacitance of a parallel plate capacitor

$$C = \frac{\varepsilon a}{d}$$

C = capacitance in Farads
a = area of one of the metal plates in square metres
d = distance between the plates in metres
$\varepsilon$ = permittivity of the dielectric in Farads per metre

### Charge stored in a capacitor

$$Q = CV$$

Q = stored charge in coulombs.

The charge stored on a capacitor in coulombs is proportional to its capacitance and to the voltage to which it is charged. The measure of capacitance is how much charge it can store per volt. The charge stored is actually the charge difference between the plates. The positive plate gains a net charge of 1/2Q and the negative plate loses 1/2Q.

### Energy stored in a capacitor

$$\text{Energy} = \frac{1}{2}CV^2$$

One may think that if Q coulombs are stored at a voltage V, then the energy available is $Q \times V = CV^2$ however this would only be true if the voltage remained at V as it would with a battery. The voltage across the capacitor falls as charge is removed. If the charge is removed at a constant current, then the voltage will fall linearly to zero and the average voltage across the capacitor will have been V/2. The energy removed is thus:

$$Q \times V/2 = CV \times V/2 = 1/2CV^2$$

## Varying the voltage across a capacitor

$$i = C\frac{dv}{dt}$$

If the voltage across the capacitor is changing, then a current must flow so that Q = CV is maintained. The current appears to flow through the capacitor but it is simply supplying or removing the charge on the plates.

## Capacitors in an ac circuit

$$X_c = \frac{1}{2\pi fC}$$

If the voltage across the capacitor is changing in a sinusoidal fashion, then the current that flows to and from the plates also has a sinusoidal waveform. The amplitude of the sinusoidal current which flows is proportional to the amplitude of the sinusoidal voltage across the capacitor. The current $I = V/X_c$ where $X_c$ is the reactance of the capacitor in ohms.

## ✋ Rules of thumb

- A capacitor stores charge and releases it when required.
- The voltage across a capacitor cannot change instantaneously.
- The current through an ideal capacitor can change instantaneously.
- In a sine wave ac circuit, the current leads the voltage by 90 degrees.
- A high value capacitor may sometimes be assumed to be a short circuit to ac.
- A capacitor blocks dc but allows ac to flow.
- A capacitor can release charge at a much higher current than that used to charge it, but cannot supply charge at a higher voltage than the voltage to which it was charged.

## Enigma: disappearing energy

Charge and energy must be conserved. SW1 is closed and C1 is charged to 10V. The charge of the capacitor is then 100 microcoulombs and the energy is 500 microjoules. SW1 is then opened and SW2 closed. Charge must be conserved and the voltage must be the same across each capacitor, consequently the resulting voltage must be 10/2 = 5V as the resulting total capacitance is 20uF. The energy on the parallel combination of capacitors is thus $CV^2/2$ =250 microjoules. Where did the other 250 microjoules go?

*Solution*

The energy is actually dissipated in the resistance of the wire, switch and the losses of the capacitor. Whenever charge is moved from one place to another in this fashion, energy must be used. If 500 microjoules is to be stored on C1, then the battery has to supply 1000 microjoules. 500 are used to transfer the energy from the battery to C1. Energy may be transferred with minimum loss however via an inductor.

**Equivalent circuit of a capacitor**

C        = the nominal value of the capacitor
Delta C = the change in capacitance due to temperature, dc voltage or frequency
L        = the inductance of the leads, metallization and the winding
ESR      = the equivalent series resistance of the leads and the metallization
CDA      = the dielectric absorption
RI       = insulation resistance (of the dielectric)
RP       = dielectric polarization resistance

### *Delta C*
The value of a capacitor changes with changes in temperature and may be up to 10,000 parts per million per degree Celsius (1%). It may increase or decrease in value depending upon the type of capacitor.

### *L*
The stray inductance of a capacitor causes it to be reduced in effectiveness at high frequencies. At the capacitor's resonant frequency, the reactance $X_L = 2\pi fL$ of the stray inductance is equal to the capacitive reactance $Xc = 1/2\pi fC$. With electrolytic capacitors, the resonant frequency may be in the order of 1MHz. With ceramic capacitors it is very much higher. If a capacitor is supplied with short leads it suggests that its stray inductance is even lower than the inductance of long leads.

### *ESR*
The equivalent series resistance of a capacitor causes it to dissipate heat when the current becomes significant. This is why a maximum ripple current is quoted for electrolytic capacitors.

### *RI*
The insulation resistance of a capacitor causes a leakage current to flow which may be a problem when the capacitor is used in a high impedance circuit such as a low frequency filter in the feedback circuit of an op-amp. Electrolytic capacitors have significant leakage currents.

### *CDA*
Dielectric absorption is where charge as absorbed into the dielectric which cannot be removed as quickly as the charge stored on the plates of the capacitor due to the dielectric polarization resistance RP in series. The effect can be thought of as charge carriers penetrated into the body of the dielectric which have to flow through a very high resistance path in order to be extracted from the capacitor. The time constant of CDA and RP may be a few milliseconds.

## Dissipation factor (tan $\delta$ )

$$\text{Tan}\delta = \frac{\text{ESR}}{X_c}$$

$$X_c = \frac{1}{\omega C}$$

Is the ratio of the ESR to the reactance of the capacitor $1/2\pi fC$ ($=1/\omega C$) measured at a specified frequency. It enables capacitors of different types to be compared in terms of their self-heating characteristics. The lower the tan $\delta$ the better.

### dv/dt of a capacitor

Is a measure of a capacitor's ability to survive pulses of current. If the voltage across a capacitor is increased linearly from one value to another, then a current will flow to provide the charge required on the plates to satisfy the equation Q=C x voltage increase. The current is equal to C dv/dt. The metallized plates and the connections from the leads to the plates must be able to carry the current without rupturing. If the actual maximum pulse of current which a capacitor could withstand was quoted, a different value would have to be quoted for each value of capacitance. By quoting dv/dt, the capacitor manufacturers are able to state one value for a particular group of capacitors. The user may then calculate the maximum current a capacitor can withstand by i = C dv/dt.

### Self healing phenomenon

The plates of a metallized film capacitor are constructed by vacuum depositing a thin metal layer onto the dielectric film. If during the operation of a metallized film capacitor there is a breakdown of the dielectric film material due to an over-voltage or a manufacturing defect, a high fault current will flow through the "puncture" in the dielectric. This causes the metallized layer around the puncture to overheat and fuse open circuit. The puncture in the dielectric is effectively isolated from the remainder of the capacitor. This phenomenon is termed "self-healing" Each time a defect in the capacitor self-heals, the effective area of the plates is reduced; this results in a gradual reduction in capacitance over the life of the capacitor.

# Uses of a capacitor
## Energy storage or smoothing

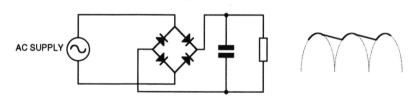

The capacitor receives energy during conduction of the diodes when the ac supply voltage is near the peak of its waveform. It releases the energy to the resistor when the diodes are not conducting and helps create a much smoother dc voltage across the resistor which is desirable for use as a dc power supply to electronic circuits. The capacitor will also help suppress over-voltage transients which may occur on the ac supply.

## AC coupling and dc blocking

The capacitor provides a low impedance ac coupling from one circuit stage to another but blocks dc from flowing. In the circuit above, TR1 is an infra-red transistor which receives pulses of infra-red light from a tv remote control unit. A positive pulse of voltage appears at the emitter each time an infra-red pulse is received. There is also a dc voltage present at the emitter. The op-amp IC1 has been configured to amplify the voltage pulse. If the emitter of TR1 was connected directly to pin 3 of the op amp, it would amplify the dc also and the op amp would go into positive saturation. The capacitor C1 couples the pulse to IC1 but blocks the dc.

---

### 👍 Rule of thumb

- The reactance of the capacitor at the lowest frequency it has to couple must be equal to the total resistance in series with the capacitor.

In order to find the total resistance in series with the capacitor:
1. Look at each capacitor lead in turn.
2. Determine how many paths there are from one lead of the capacitor.
3. Trace along each path and add up the resistances as you go along until you come to a low impedance point such as a dc rail or a low impedance output such as an op amp output.
4. Place the resistances of all the paths in parallel and calculate the total.
5. Repeat the procedure for the other capacitor lead.

6. Add the two totals.

The total resistance at the left hand lead of C1 is zero as the emitter of TR1 is a low impedance. The total resistance on the right hand lead is R4 as pin 3 of IC1 is a very high impedance.

**De-coupling**

Circuits connected to the same dc power supply rails may interfere with each other. This is because the copper wire or tracks of the power supply rails have resistance and inductance and when pulses of current flow through them, a voltage drop occurs. A pulse of current drawn by one circuit may consequently cause a dip in the supply rail feeding another circuit and cause it to malfunction. A de-coupling capacitor provides a local source of energy for a circuit stage which demands pulses of current and reduces the voltage dips in the dc supply rails thereby de-coupling that part of the circuit from the rest.

In the circuit above, a 555 timer is configured as a pulse generator (shown in the dotted box.) It is connected to the same 10V dc rail as the infra-red high-gain receiver circuit. All the copper tracks of the printed circuit board will have resistance and inductance but the drawing shows Rx, Ry, Lx, and Ly of the dc power supply tracks only. C3 de-couples the 555 circuit from IC1 circuit because it supplies the pulses of current required by IC2 with minimal dip in the 10V rail. If C3 was not present, the pulses of current would flow from the dc power supply and through Lx, Ly, Rx and Ry causing a transient voltage drop across them. The disturbance would appear across the supply to the IC1 circuit and would interfere with it.

**Low pass filter**

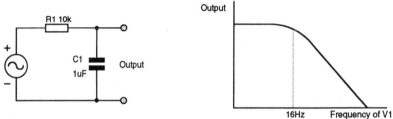

If a resistor is connected in series with a capacitor as shown, the combination acts as a low-pass filter having a cut-off frequency equal to $1/2\pi RC$. In the example above, the cut-off frequency is approximately 16Hz.

## High pass filter

If a resistor is connected in series with a capacitor as shown, the combination acts as a high-pass filter having a cut-off frequency equal to $1/2\pi RC$. In the example above, the cut-off frequency is approximately 16Hz.

# EMI suppression capacitors

EMI (electro-magnetic interference) may be generated by electrical appliances.  This electrical "noise" may interfere with other electrical or electronic equipment and cause it to malfunction.  There are standards in force which state the maximum levels of EMI which may be generated by different types of appliances.  The subject which considers the interaction of appliances in this respect is called  electro-magnetic compatibility (EMC) (see chapter 6).

Capacitor manufacturers have introduced a range of capacitors which have been specifically designed  to reduce the effects of EMI generated by electrical appliances.  The capacitors considered in this section are mainly used to reduce the interference being transmitted via the mains supply.

## Class X capacitors

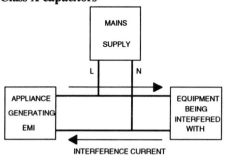

If a mains powered appliance is not earthed and is well separated from earthed equipment, then conducted EMI, generated by the appliance can only interfere with other equipment by an interference current flowing down one mains conductor and returning via the other mains conductor.  This is termed differential mode interference.

If a capacitor is connected across the mains supply at the appliance which is generating the EMI, then the differential mode interference current is offered an alternative path.  Less of the interference current will therefore flow to the other equipment .

Capacitors which are designed to be applied in this way are termed class X capacitors.  Class X capacitors are suitable for use in situations where failure of the capacitor would not lead to danger of electric shock to anyone using the appliance.

There are two classes of X capacitors,  X1 and X2.

### *Class X1   ( > 1.2kV )*
High grade capacitors which are designed to be used in applications where transient voltages may occur on the mains supply which may exceed 1.2kV peak.

### *Class X2   ( < 1.2kV )*
General purpose grade capacitors which are designed to be used in applications where transient voltages will be less than or equal to 1.2kV peak.

### *Mnemonics*
Class X capacitors are across  ( a cross X) the mains supply.
Class X1 is No1 grade therefore > 1.2kV   (1 is higher ranking than 2).

**Class Y capacitors**

If an appliance has a metal case which is earthed or has metal parts which are earthed, then there will be stray capacitances between the electrical circuitry and the earthed metal parts. Interference currents can then flow through the stray capacitances, travel along the earth conductor to other equipment, flow through the stray capacitances of that equipment and return to the appliance via the live and neutral conductors. This type of conducted interference is termed common-mode interference.

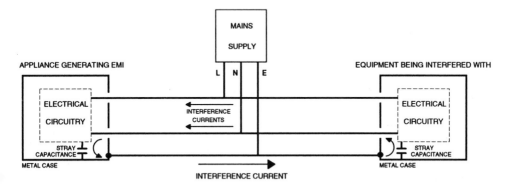

If two capacitors are connected, one between the live and earth, and the other between neutral and earth at the appliance, then the common-mode interference currents are offered an alternative path. Less of the common-mode interference currents will flow to the other equipment.

If the earth wire to the metal case of the appliance became disconnected however, then one of the Y capacitors forms a direct connection between live and the metal case. If someone touched the metal case of the appliance, they may complete a circuit to earth. The value of the Y capacitor must be such that the maximum leakage current which will flow to earth is well below the value which may cause electric shock. A figure standardized for household equipment and portable tools is <0.5mA. If the Y capacitor failed to short circuit when the earth wire was disconnected, the metal case of the appliance would be directly connected to the live conductor and would expose the user to electric shock. It is for this reason that the electrical and mechanical safety margins are increased in the design of class Y capacitors. The manufacturers are very careful not to state that the capacitor will never fail to short circuit, however the inference is that the probability that it will fail to short circuit is remote.

## Capacitor value marking systems

Some capacitor manufacturers make life easy and mark the value as it would be written i.e.:

**10uF , 5%, 100V**

European manufacturers tend to use a comma instead of the decimal point i.e. 3.3uF would be written **3,3uF**

Most manufacturers seem to have adopted the convention; value first, then tolerance, then voltage. The following table gives examples of the different methods of marking.

| MARKING | ACTUAL VALUE | NOTES |
|---------|--------------|-------|
| 102K 100 | 1000 picofarads, 10%, 100V | The first 3 digits are in the format of the resistor colour code i.e. 10 and two 0's = 1000 the value being number of picofarads |
| 0.01/5/250 | 0.01 microfarad, 5%, 250V | |
| 4n7 J 2000 | 4.7 nanofarads, 5%, 2000V | Equivalent to 4700 picofarads |
| 0,47 J 100 | 0.47 microfarads, 5%, 100V | |
| 1.0K100 | 1 microfarad, 10%, 100V | |

Some manufacturers use a convention of code letters to indicate the capacitor's tolerance.

| CODE LETTER | TOLERANCE |
|-------------|-----------|
| A | ±0.05% |
| B | ±0.1% |
| C | ±0.25% |
| D | ±0.5% |
| F | ±1% |
| G | ±2% |
| J | ±5% |
| K | ±10% |
| M | ±20% |
| N | ±30% |
| Q | -10%, +30% |
| T | -10%, +50% |
| S | -20%, +50% |
| Z | -20%, +80% |

# Capacitor selection chart

| CAPACITOR TYPE | CERAMIC NPO (COG) | CERAMIC X7R | CERAMIC Z5U | SILVER MICA | ALUMINIUM ELECTROLYTIC | TANTALUM |
|---|---|---|---|---|---|---|
| CON-STRUCTION | Thin metal layer deposited on ceramic plates | Thin metal layer deposited on ceramic plates | Thin metal layer deposited on ceramic plates | Layer of silver is applied to either side of thin mica sheet | The dielectric is an oxide layer which formed on the aluminium plates by electro-chemical action | Porous Tantalum pellet with electrolyte filling |
| ADVANTAGES | Very low temperature co-efficient | | High capacitance for medium size. Low cost | Very high stability Very high precision Good pulse handling | High capacitance for small physical size Low cost | High capacitance for small physical size Low cost. Lower leakage current than aluminium |
| DIS-ADVANTAGES | Limited capacitance range Higher values are high cost | | Poor temperature co-efficient | High Cost Large size | Limited lifetime especially at high temperature High leakage current | Limited lifetime especially at high temperature Higher cost than aluminium |
| CAPACITANCE RANGE AVAILABLE | 1.8pF to 0.47uF | 10pF to 1uF | 10pF to 2.2uF | 2.2pF to 0.01uF | 1uF to 470,000uF | 0.1uF to 100uF |
| VOLTAGES AVAILABLE | 50 to 200V | 50 to 200V | 50 to 100V | 100 to 400V | 6.3V to 400V | 6.3V to 50V |
| TOLERANCES AVAILABLE | ±5%, ±10% | ±10%, ±20% | ±10%, ±20% | ±1% | ±20%, -10 +20% | ±10%, 20% |
| TEMPERATURE COEFFICIENT | 0 to ±30 ppm / °C | ±1000 ppm / °C | ±10,000 ppm / °C | -20 to +100 ppm / °C | +1000 to +10,000 ppm / °C | +1000 ppm / °C |
| MANUFAC-TURERS | Kemet, Philips, Thomson, KVX - Kyrocera, Panasonic, Siemens | Philips, Thomson, KVX - Kyrocera, Panasonic, Siemens | Philips, Siemens, Kemet | Ashcroft, Iskra, Wimpey-Dubilier | Philips, Siemens, Wimpey-Dubilier | Kemet, Wimpey-Dubilier |

For film capacitors, see next page

# Film capacitor selection chart

| TYPE | FILM / FOIL | METALLIZED FILM |
|---|---|---|
| CONSTRUC-TION | Two aluminium foil electrodes separated by a dielectric of plastic film material | Thin metal layer vacuum deposited onto a dielectric film or a carrier film |
| ADVANTAGES | High insulation resistance. Good capacitance stability. Good current carrying ability | Small physical size.  Self healing ability |
| DIS-ADVANTAGES | Large physical dimensions | Lower voltage withstand capability than film/foil. Lower current carrying capability than film/foil |

| CAPACITOR TYPE | POLYCARBONATE KC | POLYESTER KT | POLYPROPYLENE KP | POLYSTYRENE KS | METALLIZED POLYCARBONATE MKC | METALLIZED POLYESTER MKT | METALLIZED POLYPROPYLENE MKP |
|---|---|---|---|---|---|---|---|
| ADVANTAGES | Good long term stability Low TC | High voltages available Good pulse handling Good long term stability | Low diss factor Excellent pulse perf Low losses Low dielectric absor. | Extremely low losses Low dielectric absor Low -ve TC | Low TC Low cost | Good self-healing | Low losses Low dielectric absorp. High insulation R |
| DIS-ADVANTAGES | - | Poor TC | Higher cost Larger size | Poor soldering perf Affected by some solvents | - | - | Higher cost Larger size |
| APPLICATIONS | General purpose Time delay | Bypassing, coupling | Pulse applications SMPS | Timers, filters, sample & hold | General Purpose | - | Sample/hold circuits Pulse applications SMPS, Hi f decoupling |
| TEMPERATURE COEFFICIENT | +150 ppm /°C | +500 ppm /°C | -200 ppm /°C | -150ppm /°C | +150ppm /°C or ±100ppm /°C | +400 ppm /°C | -200 ppm /°C |
| MANUFAC-TURERS | Roederstein KC1850 Rifa-Evox CFR Wima FKC2 & 3 | Wima FKS2 | Roederstein KP1830 Rifa-Evox PFR Wima FKP2 Philips 460,1,2,3,4 LCR PC/HV/S | Rifa-Evox SFA,SFR,SFE Suflex HS Philips 424,5,6,7 | Philips 344 Rifa-Evox CMK Wima FKC2 Roederstein MKC-1858,60,62 | Roederstein MKT Rifa-Evox MMK Siemens B32560 Philips - 365,8, 370,1,2,3 Wima MKS4 Thomson BF | Philips 378 Rifa-Evox PMR Roederstein-MKP1837,39,40,41,45,46 |

**5mm lead pitch - polycarbonate film and foil capacitors**

| MANFR | TYPE No | C VALUE | STD TOL | MAX V | MAX dv/dt | INSUL R | Tan δ | TEMP CO (0-80°C) | TEMP RANGE | MAX DIMENSIONS |
|---|---|---|---|---|---|---|---|---|---|---|
| EVOX | CFR5 | 0.01µF | ±10%, ±5%,2.5% ±2%,±1% | 63V dc 40V ac | 500V/µs | >100 GΩ | 0.4% max at 10kHz | -25 ppm / °C | -55 to +125 °C | ⌀ 0.5, 5, 7.0, 7.2, 5.5 |
| ROEDER-STEIN | KC1850 | 0.01µF | ±20%, ±10%, ±5% | 63V dc 40V ac | 1000V/µs | >500GΩ | 0.4% max at 10kHz | +25 ppm / °C | -55 to +100 °C | ⌀ 0.5, 5, 8.5, 7.2, 3.5 |
| WIMA | FKC2 | 0.01µF | ±10%, ±5%,2.5% | 100V dc 63V ac | 1000V/µs | >500GΩ | 0.4% max at 10kHz | -125 ppm / °C | -55 to +100 °C | ⌀ 0.5, 5, 9.5, 7.2, 4.5 |

**5mm lead pitch - polypropylene film and foil capacitors**

KP

| MANFR | TYPE No | C VALUE | STD TOL | MAX V | MAX dv/dt | INSUL R | Tan δ | TEMP CO (0-80°C) | TEMP RANGE | MAX DIMENSIONS |
|-------|---------|---------|---------|-------|-----------|---------|-------|------------------|------------|----------------|
| EVOX | PFR5 | 0.01µF | ±10%, ±5%,2.5% ±2%,±1% | 63V dc 40V ac | 500V/µs | >100 GΩ | 0.07% max at 10kHz | -220 ppm / °C | -55 to +85 °C | ⌀ 0.5, 5, 8.0, 7.2, 6.5 |
| ROEDER-STEIN | KC1830 | 0.01µF | ±10%, ±5%,2.5%, ±1% | 63V dc 40V ac | 1000V/µs | >500GΩ | 0.04% max at 10kHz | -125 ppm / °C | -55 to +100 °C | ⌀ 0.5, 5, 7, 7.2, 5.5 |
| WIMA | FKP2 | 0.01µF | ±10%, ±5%,2.5%, | 63V dc 40V ac | 1000V/µs | >500GΩ | 0.04% max at 10kHz | -375 ppm / °C | -55 to +85 °C | ⌀ 0.5, 5, 7, 7.2, 5.5 |

**5 mm lead pitch - metallized polycarbonate capacitors**                                  MKC

| MANFR | TYPE No | C VALUE | STD TOL | MAX V | MAX dv/dt | INSUL R | Tan δ | TEMP CO (0-80°C) | TEMP RANGE | MAX DIMENSIONS |
|---|---|---|---|---|---|---|---|---|---|---|
| EVOX | CMK5 | 0.1µF | ±20%, ±10%, ±5%,2.5% | 63V dc 40V ac | 10V/µs | >15 GΩ | 0.5% max at 10kHz | -12.5 ppm / °C | -55 to +125 °C | ⌀ 0.5, 8.0, 5, 7.2, 3.5 |
| ROEDER-STEIN | MKC1858 | 0.1µF | ±20%, ±10%, ±5% | 63V dc 40V ac | 17V/µs | >3.75GΩ | 0.5% max at 10kHz | -25 ppm / °C | -55 to +100 °C | ⌀ 0.5, 8.5, 5, 7.5, 3.5 |
| WIMA | MKC2 | 0.1µF | ±20%, ±10%, ±5% | 63V dc 40V ac | 15V/µs | >3.75GΩ | 0.5% max at 10kHz | -88 ppm / °C | -55 to +100 °C | ⌀ 0.5, 8.5, 5, 7.2, 3.5 |

**5 mm lead pitch - metallized polyester capacitors**

MKT

| MANFR | TYPE No | C VALUE | STD TOL | MAX V | MAX dv/dt | INSUL R | Tan δ | TEMP CO (0-80°C) | TEMP RANGE | MAX DIMENSIONS |
|---|---|---|---|---|---|---|---|---|---|---|
| EVOX | MMK5 | 0.01μF | ±20%, ±10%,±5%, | 250V dc 160V ac | 40V/μs | >30 GΩ | 1.2% max at 10kHz | +400 ppm / °C | -55 to +100 °C | ⌀ 0.5, 5, 6.5, 7.2, 2.5 |
| PHILIPS | 370 | 0.01μF | ±10% | 250V dc | 330V/μs | >15 GΩ | 1.3% at 10kHz | +X ppm / °C | -55 to +85 °C | ⌀ 0.6, 5.08, 6.5, 7.2, 2.5 |
| ROEDER-STEIN | MKT1817 | 0.01μF | ±20%, ±10%,±5%, | 250V dc 160V ac | 44V/μs | >7.5 GΩ | 1.5% at 10kHz | +375 ppm / °C | -55 to +100 °C | ⌀ 0.5, 5, 6.0, 7.5, 2.5 |
| SIEMENS | B32529 | 0.01μF | ±10% | 250V dc 160V ac | 250V/μs | >7.5 GΩ | 1.5% at 10kHz | +500 ppm / °C | -55 to +100 °C | ⌀ 0.5, 5, 6.5, 7.2, 2.5 |
| THOMSON | BF01 | 0.01μF | ±20%, ±10%,±5%, | 250V dc 160V ac | 110V/μs | >7.5 GΩ | 1% at 10kHz | +400 ppm / °C | -55 to +100 °C | ⌀ 0.6, 5.08, 6.5, 7.5, 2.5 |
| WIMA | MKS2 | 0.01μF | ±20%,±10% | 250V dc 160V ac | 50V/μs | - | 1.5% at 10kHz | +375 ppm / °C | -55 to +100 °C | ⌀ 0.5, 5, 7.0, 7.2, 2.5 |

Metallized polyester capacitors     **MKT**

| MANFR | TYPE No | C VALUE | STD TOL | MAX V | MAX dv/dt | INSUL R | Tan δ | TEMP CO (0-80°C) | TEMP RANGE | MAX DIMENSIONS |
|---|---|---|---|---|---|---|---|---|---|---|
| EVOX | MMK22.5 | 1μF | ±20%, ±10%,±5%, | 250V dc 160V ac | 8V/μs | >5 GΩ | 1.5% max at 10kHz | +375 ppm / °C | -55 to +100 °C | 22.5 / 16.5 / 25 / 7.5 / ⌀ 0.8 |
| PHILIPS | 373 | 1μF | ±10% | 250V dc 160V ac | -/μs | >10 GΩ | 1.5% max at 10kHz | +X ppm / °C | -55 to +85 °C | 22.5 / 17.5 / 26 / 8.5 / ⌀ 0.8 |
| ROEDER-STEIN | MKT1822 | 1μF | ±20%, ±10%,±5%, | 250V dc 160V ac | 8V/μs | >10 GΩ | 1.5% at 10kHz | +375 ppm / °C | -55 to +100 °C | 22.5 / 16.5 / 26.5 / 8.5 / ⌀ 0.8 |
| SIEMENS | B32523 | 1μF | ±10%,±5% | 250V dc 160V ac | 4V/μs | >2.5 GΩ | 1.0% at 1kHz | +500 ppm / °C | -55 to +100 °C | 22.5 / 16.5 / 26.5 / 8.5 / ⌀ 0.8 |
| THOMSON | BT22 | 1μF | ±20%, ±10%,±5%, | 250V dc 160V ac | 9V/μs | >2.5 GΩ | 1% | +400 ppm / °C | -55 to +100 °C | 22.5 / 19.5 / 26.25 / 10 / ⌀ 0.8 |

Axial lead - metallized polyester capacitors                    MKT

| MANFR | TYPE No | C VALUE | STD TOL | MAX V | MAX dv/dt | INSUL R | Tan δ | TEMP CO (0-80°C) | TEMP RANGE | MAX DIMENSIONS |
|---|---|---|---|---|---|---|---|---|---|---|
| ARCO-TRONICS | MKT1.5 | 47nF | ±20%, | 250V dc 160V ac | 40V/µs | >30 GΩ | 1.2% max at 10kHz | +400 ppm/°C | -55 to +100 °C | 5.0  ø.65  11 |
| ISKRA | KEU1012 | 47nF | ±20% | 250V dc | 10V/µs | - | 1.0% at 1kHz | - | -40 to +85 °C | 5.5  ø0.6  14 |
| ROEDER-STEIN | MKT1813 | 47nF | ±10%,±5%, | 250V dc | 22V/µs | >30 GΩ | 0.8% at 1kHz | +375 ppm/°C | -55 to +100 °C | 6.0  ø0.7  14 |
| THOMSON | S9 13 | 47nF | ±10% | 250V dc 100V ac | - | >7.5 GΩ | 0.8% at 1kHz | +400 ppm/°C | -55 to +100 °C | 6.25  ø0.6  14.5 |

**Radial lead - metallized polypropylene capacitors**  MKP

| MANFR | TYPE No | C VALUE | STD TOL | MAX V | MAX dv/dt | INSUL R | Tan δ | TEMP CO (0-80°C) | TEMP RANGE | MAX DIMENSIONS |
|---|---|---|---|---|---|---|---|---|---|---|
| EVOX | PMR22.5 | 1µF | ±20%, ±10%,±5%, | 250V dc 160V ac | 60V/µs | >30 GΩ | 0.1% max at 10kHz | -300 ppm / °C | -55 to +85 °C | ⌀ 0.8, 22.5, 16.5, 25, 7.5 |
| PHILIPS | 378 | 1µF | ±5% | 250V dc 160V ac | 60V/µs | >100GΩ | 0.2% at 10kHz | +X ppm / °C | -55 to +85 °C | ⌀ 0.8, 27.5, 21, 31, 11 |
| ROEDER-STEIN | MKP1840 | 1µF | ±20%, ±10%,±5%, | 250V dc 160V ac | 75V/µs | >30 GΩ | 0.06% at 10kHz | -300 ppm / °C | -55 to +100 °C | ⌀ 0.8, 22.5, 18.5, 26.5, 10.5 |
| SIEMENS | B32650 | 1µF | ±10%,±5%, | 250V dc 160V ac | 25V/µs | >10 GΩ | 0.08% at 10kHz | -300 ppm / °C | -55 to +85 °C | ⌀ 0.8, 22.5, 16.5, 26.5, 10.5 |
| THOMSON | BB22 | 1µF | ±5% | 250V dc 160V ac | 195V/µs | >6 GΩ | 0.1% at 1kHz | -300 ppm / °C | up to +100 °C | ⌀ 0.8, 22.5, 21.5, 26.25, 12.5 |
| WIMA | MKP10 | 1µF | ±20%, ±10%,±5%, | 250V dc 180V ac | 65V/µs | >30 GΩ | 0.06% at 10kHz | -300 ppm / °C | -55 to +100 °C | ⌀ 0.8, 27.5, 24, 31.5, 13 |

# 3 Inductors

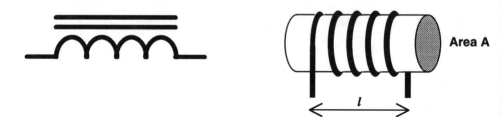

**Area A**

*Definition*

Inductance is the electrical property which exists due to presence of a magnetic field around a conductor which is carrying current. Inductance may be thought of as electrical momentum. When there is appreciable inductance in a circuit it makes it difficult to build up electron flow or current quickly, but once the current is established, inductance makes it difficult to stop quickly. A single straight piece of wire has inductance although this is only in the order of 10nH per foot. Inductance may be increased by winding wire into a coil and may be increased substantially by winding the coil around a magnetic material such as iron.

Inductance is increased in proportion to the number of turns squared.

**Inductance of a long coil**

$$L = \frac{\mu N^2 A}{l}$$

L = inductance in Henrys
A = cross sectional area of the coil in square metres
$l$ = length of the coil in metres
$\mu$ = magnetic permeability of the coil's core ($=4\pi \times 10^{-7}$ for air)

This formula is only approximate because it assumes that all the magnetic flux lines link all the turns of the coil. In practice some of the flux lines fail to link some of the turns near the ends of the coil.

If the length of the coil is 10x its diameter, then the true inductance is 4% less than that given by the formula. If the length is 4x the diameter, the true inductance is 10% less than the formula.

**Energy stored in an inductor**

$$\text{Energy} = \frac{1}{2} L i^2$$

An inductor may be thought of as "storing" current (charge which is moving) compared to a capacitor which stores stationary charge. The energy is actually stored in the magnetic field and is proportional to the current squared.

## Current build-up in an inductor

When the switch SW1 is in the position shown, V1 is connected to the inductor L1. Current builds up linearly according to the equation:

$$di/dt = V1/L1$$

After a while the current has built up and the switch is thrown over to the other position which connects L1 to the battery V2. The current cannot stop and continues to flow into V2. The battery V2 is forcing the current to stop and the current starts to linearly reduce according to the equation:

$$di/dt = V2 / L1$$

The current does not suddenly change its value, but starts to ramp down in magnitude at a rate of change dictated by the new battery voltage it is connected to. It should be mentioned that in practice, the switch should instantly change from one position to the other without a break.

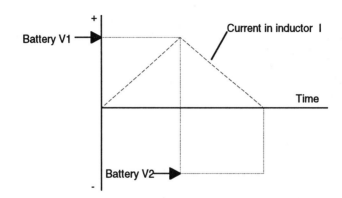

## Inductor in an ac circuit

$$X_L = 2\pi fL$$

If the voltage across the inductor is changing in a sinusoidal fashion at a frequency f, then the current that flows also has a sinusoidal waveform. The amplitude of the sinusoidal current is proportional to the amplitude of the sinusoidal voltage across the inductor. The current $I = V/X_L$ where $X_L$ is the reactance of the inductor in ohms.

### Rules of thumb

- Inductance may be thought of as storing current (electrons which are moving).
- The current in an inductor cannot change instantly.
- The voltage across an inductor can change instantly and will do so to try and keep the current through it constant.
- An inductor can receive energy from a circuit which has a low dc voltage supply and can then release the energy at a much higher voltage. It can not release the energy at a higher current than the final value the current was when it received the energy.
- In an ac circuit, the current lags the voltage by 90 degrees.
- The reactance of an inductor is $2\pi f L$, where f is the frequency of the supply.

# Uses of an inductor

## AC blocking

A pure inductor has a high impedance at high frequencies but allows dc to pass without attenuation, consequently it may be considered the opposite of a capacitor. An inductor is often used to block the conduction of high frequency interference into an item of equipment. An inductor used in this fashion is sometimes referred to as a high frequency "choke".

## di/dt limiting

When a semiconductor is used to switch a high-power, low-inductance load such as a heating element, there may be a very high rate of increase of current when the device is turned on. High power semiconductors require a finite time to fully turn on. If the current through the device increases too quickly, it may "crowd" into one area of the silicon chip and cause overheating and destruction of the device. An inductor may be used in series with the device to limit the rate of rise of the current (di/dt) to less than the maximum di/dt rating of the semiconductor device. In the example opposite, L1 limits the di/dt to $240 \times 1.414/10^4 = 3.4$ Amps per microsecond (worst-case).

## Power conversion

When current flows in an inductor, energy is stored in the magnetic field around it. This energy may be released at a higher or lower voltage than the voltage which was used in the process of building up the current. Consequently power may be converted from one voltage to another. In the example opposite, TR1 is turned hard-on and current builds up in L1 at the rate of 50V/L1. When TR1 is turned off, the current in L1 continues to flow through D1 into C1. By choosing the values of L1 and C1 and arranging for the appropriate on and off times of TR1, the output voltage may be boosted to 100V dc.

## Resonate with a capacitor

The circuit opposite is a tuned amplifier. It has the highest gain at one particular frequency; the resonant frequency of L1 and C2. At this frequency, the reactance of the inductor L1 ($2\pi f L1$) exactly equals the reactance of the capacitor C2 ($1/2\pi f C2$). At the resonant frequency, the combination of L1 and C2 presents a very high ac impedance to TR1's collector. The ac output voltage is therefore at a maximum.

# Transformers

A transformer converts electrical energy at one ac voltage to another (usually different) ac voltage at the same frequency. The winding which is energized is called the primary and the winding or windings which receive energy from the primary are called secondaries. A transformer may be specifically designed to transform power, voltage, or current but the same basic concepts apply.

### The perfect transformer

The perfect transformer is 100% efficient. It transforms an ac voltage applied to the primary to an ac voltage at the secondary in exact proportion to the turns ratio between the primary and the secondary. The output voltage is not affected by the current drawn.

$$\text{Output voltage} = \text{Input voltage} \times \frac{\text{Seconary turns}}{\text{Primary turns}}$$

In practice, a transformer is not perfect due to losses in the copper wire and the iron core. Its output voltage is affected by the current drawn due to voltage drops in the copper wire and voltage drops in the leakage reactances.

### Transformer equation

$$\text{Induced voltage} = 4.44\,N\,f\Phi$$

N = number of turns
f = frequency
Φ = magnetic flux

### 👍 Rules of thumb

- Flux is determined by: a) the applied voltage,
  b) the frequency,
  c) the number of primary turns.
- The flux is not affected by load current.
- The magnetizing current is determined by the core construction; it must adjust so as to produce a flux to give an induced voltage equal to the applied voltage.
- A transformer may be used on a higher frequency.
- It may not be used on a lower frequency.
- A transformer on no-load is an inductance (magnetizing) in parallel with a high value resistance (core losses).
- A transformer is most efficient when core losses = copper losses.

**Transformer equivalent circuit**

## Copper losses
When current is drawn from the secondary, there are voltage drops generated in the resistance of the copper wire of the windings. Energy is lost in heat and the secondary voltage falls from the value it would be in a perfect transformer. The copper losses in the primary may be represented by a resistor, Rp, in the transformer's equivalent circuit.

## Core losses
Energy is lost in the magnetic core of a transformer due to eddy currents and hysteresis. The losses may be represented by a resistor, Rc, in the equivalent circuit.

## Magnetizing inductance
When no current is being drawn from the secondary, the primary appears as an inductance which has a reactance (Xm) at the frequency of the supply to which it is connected. A current is drawn from the supply due to Xm and is called the magnetizing current.

## Leakage inductances
Some of the magnetic flux produced by the primary current does not link with the secondary winding. It is termed leakage flux and may be equated to an inductance called the primary leakage inductance. At the supply frequency it will have a reactance, Xp, and will cause a voltage drop in the secondary voltage when current is drawn. The secondary also has a leakage inductance which will give a reactance, Xs. This will also cause a voltage drop when current is drawn. The leakage effects are mainly in air and so the leakage inductances will not saturate as the current in the windings increases.

## Inter-winding capacitance
There will be stray capacitance between the primary and secondary windings due to the fact that they are close to each other. A current will flow through this capacitance although generally it is a common mode effect which will cause leakage currents to earth in mains transformer systems. Modern mains transformers have their primary and secondary windings on separate bobbins which increases leakage inductances but reduces inter-winding capacitance.

**Difference between a voltage transformer and a current transformer**

Although current transformers are specially designed for the purpose, in theory, there is no difference between a current transformer and a voltage transformer. It is the way they are connected which dictates their type.

The circuit opposite employs an isolating transformer T1 with 1:1 turns ratio. The impedance of the voltage source V1 is 1 ohm. The 100 ohm load resistor R1, causes a current to flow of approximately 1A. 1A also flows in the primary. It is the transformer and its load which are dictating the current which flows from the source. T1 is connected as a voltage transformer as it is presenting the source voltage to the resistor R1.

The same transformer is now connected with its primary in series with a 100 ohm resistor. The secondary has a 1 ohm load. It is now the 100 ohm resistor R2 which is dictating the current flowing from the voltage source as the impedance presented by the transformer is much lower than R2. T1 is now connected as a current transformer as it is transforming the current set by R2 across to the resistor R1.

A current transformer can be removed from a system and replaced with a short circuit and the remaining system will be unaffected. This cannot be done with a voltage transformer.

In practice, current transformers are designed with a low number of turns on the primary (often 1/2 turn) and a much larger number of turns on the secondary. They are used to enable an ammeter of say 1A full scale to measure many hundreds of amps in a circuit where the current is dictated by other devices in series with the transformer and not the transformer itself.

# 4 Semiconductors

14 PIN DIL      TO-18      TO-39      TO-3

TO-92    TO-126      TO-202      TO-220    TO-218

Semiconductors is the collective term for electronic devices which are constructed from semiconductor material. Semiconductor material is processed from a non-conducting material such as silicon and after processing it becomes conductive with a resistivity in between that of a metallic conductor (such as copper) and an insulator such as ceramic. Semiconductor materials of different types may be combined to form devices such as transistors, diodes, thyristors, and integrated circuits.

This section contains basic data and concepts related to semiconductor devices which are in common use. The cross-reference tables at the end of each sub-section include devices which have evolved as "industry standard" parts. They have been selected as being the most common devices which appear in electronic component distributors' catalogues.

In general, semiconductor devices are less linear than passive components such as resistors and capacitors i.e. the current in a semiconductor device does not linearly follow the voltage applied across it.

Semiconductor devices are electrically less rugged than passive components. Semiconductors may be destroyed by too much heat during the soldering process and may be damaged by static electricity during handling.

# Semiconductor prefixes

A common problem experienced by engineers is to identify the manufacturer of a semiconductor device from its type number only. The following table gives an alphabetical listing of letter combinations and the manufacturers of the devices having type numbers commencing with those letters.

| | |
|---|---|
| **A** | AMD |
| **ACF** | GENERAL INSTRUMENT |
| **ACP** | ITT |
| **ACR** | MEDL |
| **ACVP** | ITT |
| **AD** | ANALOG DEVICES |
| **ADC** | ANALOG DEVICES,HARRIS SEMICONDUCTOR,GENERAL INSTRUMENT, ITT |
| **AH** | NATIONAL SEMICONDUCTOR |
| **AM** | ADVANCED MICRO DEVICES, AMD |
| **AMU** | ITT |
| **AN** | PANASONIC (MATSUSHITA) |
| **APU** | ITT |
| **AR** | GENERAL INSTRUMENT |
| **ARS** | GENERAL INSTRUMENT |
| **ASC** | ITT |
| **AW** | GENERAL INSTRUMENT |
| **AY** | GENERAL INSTRUMENT |
| | |
| **B** | FAGOR, GENERAL INSTRUMENT |
| **BA** | FAGOR |
| **BAT** | ITT,PHILIPS COMPONENTS |
| **BAV** | ITT, PHILIPS |
| **BAW** | ITT |
| **BAX** | ITT |
| **BB** | ITT |
| **BY** | FAGOR |
| **BYM** | GENERAL INSTRUMENT |
| **BYV** | GENERAL INSTRUMENT |
| **BYW** | GENERAL INSTRUMENT |
| **BDM** | ANALOG DEVICES |
| **BSS** | SIEMENS |
| **BT** | PHILIPS COMPONENTS |
| **BTA** | THOMSON |
| **BTB** | THOMSON |
| **BTW** | THOMSON |
| **BUD** | THOMSON |
| **BUF** | THOMSON |
| **BUH** | THOMSON |
| **BUL** | THOMSON, MOTOROLA |
| **BUR** | THOMSON |
| **BUT** | THOMSON |
| **BUV** | THOMSON |
| **BUW** | THOMSON |
| **BUX** | THOMSON |
| **BUZ** | SIEMENS,HARRIS SEMICONDUCTOR, THOMSON |
| **BY** | THOMSON |
| **BYT** | THOMSON |
| **BYV** | THOMSON |
| **BYW** | THOMSON |
| **BYX** | THOMSON |
| **BZV** | THOMSON |

| | |
|---|---|
| **BZW** | THOMSON |
| **BZX** | THOMSON |
| **BZY** | THOMSON |

| | |
|---|---|
| **C** | GENERAL INSTRUMENT,AMD |
| **CA** | HARRIS SEMICONDUCTOR,FAIRCHILD,PHILIPS COMPONENTS,INTERNATIONAL RECTIFIER |
| **CAP** | ITT |
| **CB** | THOMSON, INTERNATIONAL RECTIFIER |
| **CBC** | INTERNATIONAL RECTIFIER |
| **CC** | GENERAL INSTRUMENT |
| **CCD** | ITT |
| **CCU** | ITT |
| **CD** | NATIONAL SEMICONDUCTOR,HARRIS SEMICONDUCTOR, |
| **CCD** | FAIRCHILD |
| **CDG** | TELEDYNE |
| **CDP** | HARRIS SEMICONDUCTOR |
| **CF** | GENERAL INSTRUMENT |
| **CG** | STA, GENERAL INSTRUMENT |
| **CK** | GENERAL INSTRUMENT |
| **CL** | GENERAL INSTRUMENT |
| **CLK** | ITT |
| **CMP** | PRECISION MONOLITHICS INCORPORATED |
| **CN** | THOMSON |
| **CP** | ITT,GENERAL INSTRUMENT |
| **CPA** | INTERNATIONAL RECTIFIER |
| **CPAT** | INTERNATIONAL RECTIFIER |
| **CPT** | INTERNATIONAL RECTIFIER |
| **CPU** | INTERNATIONAL RECTIFIER |
| **CPV** | INTERNATIONAL RECTIFIER |
| **CPY** | INTERNATIONAL RECTIFIER |
| **COM** | STA |
| **CR** | SILICONIX |
| **CS** | INTERNATIONAL RECTIFIER, NIPPON ELECTRIC CO |
| **CSP** | ITT |
| **CT** | PLESSEY, INTERNATIONAL RECTIFIER |
| **CTC** | INTERNATIONAL RECTIFIER |
| **CVPU** | ITT |
| **CX** | SONY |
| **CXA** | SONY |
| **CXB** | SONY |
| **CXD** | SONY |
| **CXK** | SONY |
| **CXL** | SONY |

| | |
|---|---|
| **D** | SILICONIX, HARRIS SEMICONDUCTOR, THOMSON |
| **DAC** | GENERAL INSTRUMENT,DAT,ANALOG DEVICES,PRECISION MONOLITHICS INCORPORATED,NATIONAL SEMICONDUCTOR |
| **DAS** | ANALOG DEVICES |
| **DB** | THOMSON |
| **DC** | THOMSON |
| **DF** | GENERAL INSTRUMENT, INTERNATIONAL RECTIFIER |
| **DG** | SILICONIX, GENERAL INSTRUMENT, HARRIS SEMICONDUCTOR |
| **DH** | NATIONAL SEMICONDUCTOR |
| **DM** | NATIONAL SEMICONDUCTOR |

| | |
|---|---|
| **DMA** | ITT |
| **DN** | NATIONAL SEMICONDUCTOR, PANASONIC, NIPPON ELECTRIC CO |
| **DNO-** | NIPPON ELECTRIC CO |
| **DP** | NATIONAL SEMICONDUCTOR, INTERNATIONAL RECTIFIER |
| **DPU** | ITT |
| **DS** | NATIONAL SEMICONDUCTOR |
| **DSC** | ANALOG DEVICES |
| **DTI** | ITT |
| **DTM** | ANALOG DEVICES |
| **DTV** | THOMSON |
| **DVR** | PRECISION MONOLITHICS INCORPORATED |
| | |
| **E** | THOMSON |
| **EDF** | GENERAL INSTRUMENT |
| **EF** | THOMSON |
| **EFG** | THOMSON |
| **EFR** | THOMSON |
| **EGL** | GENERAL INSTRUMENT |
| **EGP** | GENERAL INSTRUMENT |
| **EL** | ELAN |
| **EM** | ITT |
| **EMUS** | THOMSON |
| **EP** | PANASONIC (MATSUSHITA) |
| **ER** | GENERAL INSTRUMENT |
| **ESM** | THOMSON |
| **ETC** | THOMSON |
| **ETL** | THOMSON |
| | |
| **F** | FAIRCHILD |
| **FA** | NEC |
| **FAOH** | NEC |
| | |
| **FB** | FAGOR |
| **FBP** | FAGOR |
| **FBU** | FAGOR |
| **FC** | NEC |
| **FCD** | FAIRCHILD |
| **FCM** | FAIRCHILD |
| **FCS** | FAIRCHILD |
| **FE** | GENERAL INSTRUMENT |
| **FEP** | GENERAL INSTRUMENT |
| **FES** | GENERAL INSTRUMENT |
| **FIP** | NEC |
| **FLC** | FAIRCHILD |
| **FLV** | FAIRCHILD |
| **FM** | NEC |
| **FNA** | FAIRCHILD |
| **FND** | FAIRCHILD |
| **FPA** | FAIRCHILD |
| **FPE** | FAIRCHILD |
| **FPT** | FAIRCHILD |
| **FSOH** | NEC |
| **FZOH** | NEC |
| | |
| **G** | SILICONIX, GENERAL INSTRUMENT |
| **GAL** | THOMSON, LATTICE SEMICONDUCTOR |
| **GBPC** | GENERAL INSTRUMENT |
| **GBU** | GENERAL INSTRUMENT |
| **GE** | HARRIS SEMICONDUCTOT |

| | |
|---|---|
| **GEM** | HARRIS SEMICONDUCTOR CO |
| **GES** | HARRIS SEMICONDUCTOR |
| **GI** | GENERAL INSTRUMENT |
| **GL** | GENERAL INSTRUMENT |
| **GLL** | GENERAL INSTRUMENT |
| **GP** | GENERAL INSTRUMENT |
| **GPP** | GENERAL INSTRUMENT |
| **GS** | THOMSON |
| **GSC** | THOMSON |
| **GSD** | THOMSON |
| **GT** | SESCOSEM |
| | |
| **H** | THOMSON,FAIRCHILD, HARRIS SEMICONDUCTOR, HITACHI |
| **HA** | HITACHI,HARRIS SEMICONDUCTOR |
| **HAL** | ITT |
| **HB** | HITACHI |
| **HD** | HITACHI |
| **HE** | INTERNATIONAL RECTIFIER |
| **HEF** | PHILIPS COMPONENTS |
| **HBF** | THOMSON |
| **HC** | HARRIS SEMICONDUCTOR,MHS |
| **HCC** | HARRIS SEMICONDUCTOR |
| **HCF** | HARRIS SEMICONDUCTOR, THOMSON |
| **HCPL** | HEWL |
| **HCTL** | HEWL |
| **HD** | HARRIS SEMICONDUCTOR,HITACHI |
| **HDSP** | HEWL |
| **HEDS** | HEWL |
| **HEMT** | HEWL |
| **HFA** | HARRIS SEMICONDUCTOR, INTERNATIONAL RECTIFIER |
| **HFBR** | HEWL |
| **HI** | HARRIS,SEMICONDUCTOR |
| **HLCP** | HEWL |
| **HLMP** | HEWL |
| **HM** | HARRIS SEMICONDUCTOR, MHS, HITACHI |
| **HN** | HITACHI |
| **HSMP** | HEWL |
| **HSMS** | HEWL |
| **HSMX** | HEWL |
| **HSMY** | HEWL |
| **HSSR** | HEWL |
| **HTA** | THOMSON |
| **HTIL** | HEWL |
| **HV** | HARRIS SEMICONDUCTOR |
| **HXTR** | HEWL |
| | |
| **IC** | NEC |
| **ICL** | HARRIS SEMICONDUCTOR |
| **ICM** | HARRIS SEMICONDUCTOR |
| **ID** | HESMI |
| **IGT** | HARRIS SEMICONDUCTOR |
| **IH** | HARRIS SEMICONDUCTOR |
| **IL** | LITRONIX |
| **IM** | HARRIS SEMICONDUCTOR. INMOS |
| **IMS-** | THOMSON |
| **IMST** | INMOS |
| **IP** | HARRIS SEMICONDUCTOR |
| **IR** | INTERNATIONAL RECTIFIER |
| **IRC** | INTERNATIONAL RECTIFIER |

| | |
|---|---|
| **IRCC** | INTERNATIONAL RECTIFIER |
| **IRCP** | INTERNATIONAL RECTIFIER |
| **IRCZ** | INTERNATIONAL RECTIFIER |
| **IRD** | INTERNATIONAL RECTIFIER |
| **IRF** | INTERNATIONAL RECTIFIER, HARRIS SEMICONDUCTOR, THOMSON |
| **IRF-** | INTERNATIONAL RECTIFIER |
| **IRG-** | INTERNATIONAL RECTIFIER |
| **IRH-** | INTERNATIONAL RECTIFIER |
| **IRK-** | INTERNATIONAL RECTIFIER |
| **IRL-** | INTERNATIONAL RECTIFIER |
| **IRT** | ITT |
| **IS** | HARRIS SEMICONDUCTOR |
| **ISB** | THOMSON |
| **ISP** | ITT |
| **IT** | HARRIS SEMICONDUCTOR |
| **ITA** | THOMSON |
| **ITT** | ITT |
| | |
| **J** | HARRIS SEMICONDUCTOR, SILICONIX |
| **JA** | ITT |
| **JAN-** | INTERNATIONAL RECTIFIER |
| **JC** | ITT |
| | |
| **K** | INTERNATIONAL RECTIFIER |
| **KB** | GENERAL INSTRUMENT |
| **KBPC** | INTERNATIONAL RECTIFIER, MICRO ELECTRONICS |
| **KR** | STANDARD MICROSYSTEMS (US) |
| | |
| **L** | THOMSON,SILICONIX |
| **LA** | LAMBDA |
| **LCP** | THOMSON |
| **LDP** | THOMSON |
| **LD** | HARRIS SEMICONDUCTOR |
| **LF** | TEXAS INST,NATIONAL SEMICONDUCTOR,PHILIPS COMPONENTS,MOTOROLA,THOMSON |
| **LH** | NATIONAL SEMICONDUCTOR,PHILIPS COMPONENTS,SILICONIX |
| **LL** | ITT |
| **LM** | NATIONAL SEMICONDUCTOR,TEXAS INSTRUMENTS,FAIRCHILD,PHILIPS COMPONENTS,SILICONIX, LINEAR TECH, THOMSON, HARRIS |
| **LP** | HARRIS SEMICONDUCTOR CO, GENERAL INSTRUMENT,NATIONAL SEMICONDUCTOR |
| **LS** | THOMSON |
| **LT** | LINEAR TECH |
| **LTC** | LINEAR TECH |
| **LTK** | LINEAR TECH |
| **LZ** | ITT |
| | |
| **M** | THOMSON, MITSUBISHI |
| **MAB** | PHILIPS COMPONENTS |
| **MAC** | MOTOROLA |
| **MAF** | PHILIPS COMPONENTS |
| **MB** | RECTRON |
| **MBD** | MOTOROLA |
| **MBR** | GENERAL INSTRUMENT, INTERNATIONAL RECTIFIER, MOTOROLA |
| **MC** | MOTOROLA, HARRIS SEMICONDUCTOR CO, GENERAL INSTRUMENT, THOMSON,NEC |
| **MCM** | MOTOROLA |
| **MCR** | MOTOROLA |
| **MCT** | MOTOROLA |

| | |
|---|---|
| **MCU** | ITT |
| **MD** | MOTOROLA |
| **MDA** | ITT, MOTOROLA |
| **MDC** | MOTOROLA |
| **MDS** | THOMSON |
| **MEM** | HARRIS SEMICONDUCTOR CO, GENERAL INSTRUMENT |
| **MFE** | MOTOROLA |
| **MFO-** | MOTOROLA |
| **MH** | NATIONAL SEMICONDUCTOR |
| **MJ** | MOTOROLA, THOMSON, HARRIS SEMICONDUCTOR |
| **MJD** | MOTOROLA |
| **MJE** | MOTOROLA, HARRIS SEMICONDUCTOR, THOMSON |
| **MJF** | MOTOROLA |
| **MJH** | MOTOROLA |
| **MIC** | ITT |
| **MK** | MOSTEK, THOMSON, MOTOROLA |
| **ML** | PLESSEY, THOMSON |
| **MLED** | MOTOROLA |
| **MLM** | MOTOROLA |
| **MM** | NATIONAL SEMICONDUCTOR |
| **MM--** | MOTOROLA |
| **MN** | PANASONIC |
| **MOC** | MOTOROLA |
| **MOD** | SILICONIX |
| **MP** | TOSHIBA |
| **MPF** | MOTOROLA |
| **MPM** | MOTOROLA |
| **MPN** | MOTOROLA |
| **MPQ** | MOTOROLA |
| **MPG** | GENERAL INSTRUMENT |
| **MPQ** | THOMSON |
| **MPS-** | MOTOROLA |
| **MPSA** | MOTOROLA |
| **MPSH** | MOTOROLA |
| **MPSL** | MOTOROLS |
| **MPSU** | MOTOROLA |
| **MPSW** | MOTOROLA |
| **MPTE** | MOTOROLA |
| | |
| **MPX** | ANALOG DEVICES, MOTOROLA |
| **MPF** | NATIONAL SEMICONDUCTOR |
| **MPY** | BURR BROWN |
| **MR** | MOTOROLA |
| **MRD** | MOTOROLA |
| **MRF** | MOTOROLA |
| **MSD** | MOTOROLA |
| **MSE** | ITT |
| **MSM** | OKI |
| **MSP** | ITT |
| **MSS** | THOMSON |
| **MTA** | MOTOROLA |
| **MTD** | MOTOROLA |
| **MTE** | MOTOROLA |
| **MTH** | MOTOROLA, THOMSON |
| **MTM** | MOTOROLA |
| **MTP** | MOTOROLA, THOMSON |
| **MR** | FAGOR |
| **MU** | MOTOROLA |
| **MUR** | HARRIS SEMICONDUCTOR, MOTOROLA |

| | |
|---|---|
| **MUX** | HARRIS SEMICONDUCTOR CO, GENERAL INSTRUMENT |
| **MV** | MOTOROLA |
| **MVAM** | MOTOROLA |
| **MZD** | MOTOROLA |
| | |
| **N** | PHILIPS COMPONENTS |
| **NA** | HARRIS SEMICONDUCTOR |
| **NE** | PHILIPS COMPONENTS, THOMSON |
| **NOM** | PLESSEY |
| **NP** | GENERAL INSTRUMENT |
| **NPF** | GENERAL INSTRUMENT |
| **NR** | HARRIS SEMICONDUCTOR |
| **NS** | GENERAL INSTRUMENT |
| **NSF** | GENERAL INSTRUMENT |
| **NVM** | ITT |
| | |
| **OP** | PLESSEY,PRECISION MONOLITHICS INCORPORATED |
| | |
| **P** | INTERNATIONAL RECTIFIER,AMD, GENERAL INSTRUMENT, THOMSON,HARRIS, MOTOROLA |
| **PA** | PHILIPS COMPONENTS |
| **PBL** | THOMSON |
| **PCA** | PHILIPS COMPONENTS |
| **PCB** | PHILIPS COMPONENTS |
| **PCD** | PHILIPS COMPONENTS |
| **PCF** | PHILIPS COMPONENTS |
| **PFR** | THOMSON |
| **PIC** | ITT,HARRIS SEMICONDUCTOR CO, GENERAL INSTRUMENT, UNITRODE |
| **PIP** | ITT |
| **PL** | THOMSON |
| **PLQ** | THOMSON |
| **PM** | HARRIS SEMICONDUCTOR CO, GENERAL INSTRUMENT,PRECISION MONOLITHICS INCORPORATED |
| **PNA** | PHILIPS COMPONENTS |
| **PP** | HARRIS SEMICONDUCTOR CO, GENERAL INSTRUMENT |
| **PS** | NEC |
| **PSP** | ITT |
| **PVA** | INTERNATIONAL RECTIFIER |
| **PVA-** | INTERNATIONAL RECTIFIER |
| **PVD** | INTERNATIONAL RECTIFIER |
| **PVI** | INTERNATIONAL RECTIFIER |
| **PVPU** | ITT |
| **PVR** | INTERNATIONAL RECTIFIER |
| **QFT** | TEL |
| | |
| **R** | INTERNATIONAL RECTIFIER |
| **RA** | HARRIS SEMICONDUCTOR CO, GENERAL INSTRUMENT,RAYTHEON |
| **RAY** | RAYTHEON |
| **RC** | RAYTHEON |
| **RCA** | HARRIS SEMICONDUCTOR |
| **RCR** | ITT |
| **RCT** | ITT |
| **REF** | PRECISION MONOLITHICS INCORPORATED, |
| **RF_** | HARRIS SEMICONDUCTOR |
| **RG** | GENERAL INSTRUMENT |
| **RGL** | GENERAL INSTRUMENT |
| **RGP** | GENERAL INSTRUMENT |
| **RL** | RECTRON |
| **RM** | HARRIS SEMICONDUCTOR CO, GENERAL INSTRUMENT,RAYTHEON |

| | |
|---|---|
| **RMP** | GENERAL INSTRUMENT |
| **RO** | ITT,HARRIS SEMICONDUCTOR CO, GENERAL INSTRUMENT |
| **RRF** | HARRIS SEMICONDUCTOR |
| **RS** | GENERAL INSTRUMENT |
| **RTI** | ANALOG DEVICES |
| **RUR** | HARRIS SEMICONDUCTOR |
| | |
| **S** | SIEMENS, TAG SEMICONDUCTORS, SEIKO INSTRUMENTS, INTERNATIONAL RECTIFIER |
| **SA** | PHILIPS COMPONENTS, THOMSON |
| **SAA** | PHILIPS COMPONENTS,ITT,HARRIS SEMICONDUCTOR CO, GENERAL INSTRUMENT, THOMSON |
| **SAB** | PHILIPS COMPONENTS |
| **SAC** | ANALOG DEVICES |
| **SAD** | ITT |
| **SAF** | ITT |
| **SAK** | ITT |
| **SAJ** | ITT,THOMSON |
| **SAH** | ITT |
| **SAS** | SIEMENS |
| **SB** | GENERAL INSTRUMENT |
| **SBA** | HARRIS SEMICONDUCTOR CO, GENERAL INSTRUMENT |
| **SBL** | GENERAL INSTRUMENT |
| **SBLF** | GENERAL INSTRUMENT |
| **SBP** | TEXAS INSTRUMENTS |
| **SC** | INTERNATIONAL RECTIFIER |
| **SD** | PHILIPS COMPONENTS, TELEDYNE, INTERNATIONAL RECTIFIER, ITT |
| **SDA** | THOMSON |
| **SDC** | ANALOG DEVICES |
| **SE** | PHILIPS COMPONENTS, THOMSON |
| **SFC** | SESCOSEM |
| **SG** | SILICONIX,HARRIS SEMICONDUCTOR,SILICON GENERAL, PHILIPS ,SPRAGUE, THOMSON |
| **SGL** | GENERAL INSTRUMENT |
| **SGS** | THOMSON |
| **SGT** | HARRIS SEMICONDUCTOR |
| **SH** | FAIRCHILD |
| **SHA** | ANALOG DEVICES |
| **SI** | SILICONIX |
| **SKB** | SEMIKRON |
| **SKD** | SEMIKRON |
| **SKKD** | SEMIKRON |
| **SKKH** | SEMIKRON |
| **SKKT** | SEMIKRON |
| **SL** | HARRIS SEMICONDUCTOR CO, GENERAL INSTRUMENT,PLESSEY |
| **SM** | SILICON GENERAL, THOMSON, SEMELAB |
| **SML** | SEMELAB |
| **SMM** | SILICONIX |
| **SMP** | PRECISION MONOLITHICS INCORPORATED, SILICONIX |
| **SMV** | SILICONIX |
| **SMW** | SILICONIX |
| **SMX** | ANALOG DEVICES |
| **SN** | TEXAS INSTRUMENTS |
| **SO** | THOMSON |
| **SP** | PLESSEY, INTERNATIONAL RECTIFIER, HARRIS SEMICONDUCTOR |
| **SPBM** | SILICONIX |
| **SPMF** | SILICONIX |
| **SPU** | ITT |
| **SSC-** | INTERNATIONAL RECTIFIER |

| | |
|---|---|
| **SSM** | PRECISION MONOLITHICS INCORPORATED |
| **SR** | STANDARD MICROSYSTEMS CORP |
| **SRP** | GENERAL INSTRUMENT |
| **SRX** | ANALOG DEVICES |
| **SS** | HARRIS SEMICONDUCTOR CO, GENERAL INSTRUMENT |
| **SSC** | ANALOG DEVICES |
| **SSS** | PRECISION MONOLITHICS INCORPORATED |
| **ST** | THOMSON, INTERNATIONAL RECTIFIER |
| **STF** | THOMSON |
| **STGH** | THOMSON |
| **STGP** | THOMSON |
| **STH** | THOMSON |
| **STHV** | THOMSON |
| **STK** | THOMSON |
| **STKM** | THOMSON |
| **STLT** | THOMSON |
| **STP** | THOMSON |
| **STPR** | THOMSON |
| **STPS** | THOMSON |
| **STV** | THOMSON |
| **STVH** | THOMSON |
| | |
| **SU** | PHILIPS COMPONENTS |
| **SW** | PLESSEY |
| | |
| **T** | HARRIS SEMICONDUCTOR CO, GENERAL INSTRUMENT,TRANSITRON,THOMSON, TAG, INTERNATIONAL RECTIFIER |
| **TA** | TOSHIBA |
| **TAA** | THOMSON,PHILIPS COMPONENTS,ITT,SIEMENS,FAIRCHILD |
| **TBA** | THOMSON,PHILIPS COMPONENTS,ITT,SIEMENS,FAIRCHILD, TELFUNKEN |
| **TBB** | SIEMENS |
| **TBC** | SIEMENS |
| **TBE** | SIEMENS |
| **TCA** | PHILIPS COMPONENTS,ITT,SIEMENS, TELEFUNKEN |
| **TC** | TOSHIBA, TELEDYNE |
| **TD** | TOSHIBA |
| **TDA** | PHILIPS COMPONENTS,ITT,SIEMENS,FAIRCHILD,THOMSON, TELEFUNKEN |
| **TDB** | SIEMENS,THOMSON |
| **TDC** | SIEMENS,THOMSON |
| **TDD** | PHILIPS COMPONENTS |
| **TDE** | THOMSON |
| **TDF** | THOMSON |
| **TDP** | THOMSON |
| **TEA** | PHILIPS COMPONENTS, TELEFUNKEN, THOMSON |
| **TEB** | THOMSON |
| **TEF** | THOMSON |
| **TFF** | TRANSITRON |
| **TFIR** | ITT |
| **TFPO** | ITT |
| **TGAL** | THOMSON |
| **TGDV** | THOMSON |
| **TGF** | THOMSON |
| **TH** | TOSHIBA |
| **THBT** | THOMSON |
| **THDT** | THOMSON |
| **THM** | TOSHIBA |
| **TIP** | TEXAS INSTRUMENTS, THOMSON, HARRIS SEMICONDUCTOR |
| **TF** | TRANSITRON |
| **TG** | TRANSITRON |

| | |
|---|---|
| **TGL** | GENERAL INSTRUMENT |
| **TL** | TEXAS INSTRUMENTS, THOMSON |
| **TLC** | TEXAS INSTRUMENTS, THOMSON |
| **TLG** | TOSHIBA |
| **TLN** | TOSHIBA |
| **TLO** | TOSHIBA |
| **TLP** | TOSHIBA |
| **TLS** | THOMSON |
| **TLR** | TOSHIBA |
| **TLRA** | TOSHIBA |
| **TLRC** | TOSHIBA |
| **TLS** | TOSHIBA |
| **TLSG** | TOSHIBA |
| **TLUR** | TOSHIBA |
| **TLY** | TOSHIBA |
| **TM** | TOSHIBA, THOMSON |
| **TMM** | THOMSON |
| **TMP** | TOSHIBA |
| **TMS** | TEXAS INSTRUMENTS |
| **TNG** | TRANSITRON |
| **TOSH** | TOSHIBA |
| **TP** | TELEDYNE |
| **TPQ** | SPRAGUE |
| **TPS** | TOSHIBA |
| **TPU** | ITT |
| **TOA** | TRANSITRON |
| **TODV** | THOMSON |
| **TPA** | THOMSON |
| **TPB** | THOMSON |
| **TPDV** | THOMSON |
| **TPP** | THOMSON |
| **TRAL** | THOMSON |
| **TRC** | TRANSITRON |
| **TS** | THOMSON |
| **TSA** | PHILIPS COMPONENTS |
| **TSD** | THOMSON |
| **TSDC** | ANALOG DEVICES |
| **TSFJ** | THOMSON |
| **TSFK** | THOMSON |
| **TSG** | THOMSON |
| **TSGF** | THOMSON |
| **TSGS** | THOMSON |
| **TSL** | ANALOG DEVICES |
| **TVPO** | ITT |
| **TXDV** | THOMSON |
| **TYN** | THOMSON |
| **TYP** | THOMSON |
| **TYS** | THOMSON |
| **TZ** | HARRIS SEMICONDUCTOR GENERAL INSTRUMENT |
| | |
| **U** | FAIRCHILD, TELEFUNKEN |
| **UA** | FAIRCHILD,PHILIPS COMPONENTS,TEXAS INSTRUMENTS,NATIONAL SEMICONDUCTOR, THOMSON |
| **UAA** | ITT,SIEMENS, TELEFUNKEN, THOMSON |
| **UAF** | ITT, THOMSON |
| **UC** | UNITRODE,THOMSON, LINEAR TECH |
| **UCN** | SPRAGUE |
| **UCS** | SPRAGUE |
| **UDN** | PHILIPS COMPONENTS,SPRAGUE |

| | |
|---|---|
| **UDS** | SPRAGUE |
| **UF** | GENERAL INSTRUMENT |
| **UHD** | SPRAGUE |
| **UHP** | SPRAGUE |
| **ULC** | SPRAGUE |
| **ULN** | SPRAGUE,PHILIPS COMPONENTS, THOMSON |
| **ULQ** | THOMSON |
| **ULS** | SPRAGUE |
| **UPB** | NEC |
| **UPC** | STANDARD MICROSYSTEMS, NIPPON ELECTRIC COMPANY |
| **UPD** | NEC |
| | |
| **V** | HARRIS SEMICONDUCTOR |
| **VAD** | ITT |
| **VB** | THOMSON |
| **VCU** | ITT |
| **VDU** | ITT |
| **VSP** | ITT |
| **VN** | TELEDYNE, THOMSON |
| | |
| **W** | GENERAL INSTRUMENT |
| | |
| **X** | TAG SEMICONDUCTORS |
| **XR** | EXAR |
| **Y** | TEXAS INSTRUMENTS |
| **TYF** | TOSHIBA |
| **YTFP** | TOSHIBA |
| **Z** | THOMSON, INTERNATIONAL RECTIFIER |
| **ZA** | ZETEX, TEXAS INSTRUMENTS |
| **ZAD** | ZETEX, TEXAS INSTRUMENTS |
| **ZD** | INTERNATIONAL RECTIFIER |
| **ZEL** | ZETEX,TEXAS INSTRUMENTS |
| **ZGL** | GENERAL INSTRUMENT |
| **ZGP** | GENERAL INSTRUMENT |
| **ZM** | ITT |
| **ZMM** | ITT |
| **ZMU** | ITT |
| **ZMY** | ITT |
| **ZN** | PLESSEY, FERRANTI |
| **ZPD** | ITT |
| **ZPU** | ITT |
| **ZPY** | ITT |
| **ZTE** | ITT |
| **ZTX** | ITT |
| **ZY** | ITT |
| **ZZ** | ITT |
| **ZZY** | ITT |
| | |
| **ZN** | PLESSEY, FERRANTI |
| **ZS** | FERRANTI, PLESSEY |
| | |
| **1.5KE** | SGS |

*Note:*
Intersil and RCA are now Harris
Signetics is now Philips Components
Ferranti transistors are now Zetex

**Japanese transistor prefixes**

| | |
|---|---|
| **2SA** | PNP HIGH FREQUENCY |
| **2SB** | PNP LOW FREQUENCY |
| **2SC** | NPN HIGH FREQUENCY |
| **2SD** | NPN LOW FREQUENCY |
| **2SH** | UNIJUNCTION |
| **2SJ** | P CHANNEL FET |
| **2SK** | N CHANNEL FET |

Occasionally the "2S" is omitted thus a PNP high frequency transistor may be marked "A1279" instead of "2SA1279".

# Diodes

The diode is a two terminal semiconductor device which conducts current readily when the anode is made positive with respect to the cathode (forward biased). A very small current flows when the cathode is made positive with respect to the anode (reverse biased).

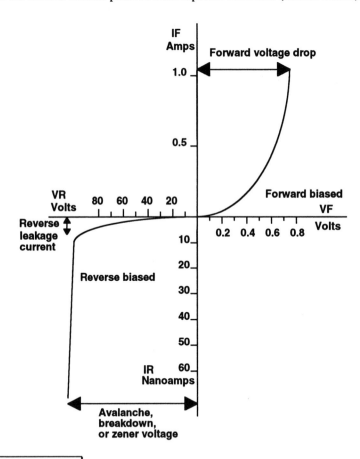

| $\text{\textcircled{$\unicode{x261D}$}}$ **Rules of thumb** |
|---|

- A diode has a constant forward voltage drop = 0.6V.
- The reverse leakage current of a signal diode is approx 25nA at 25V.
- The forward drop reduces by 2.5mV for every 1 degree C rise.
- The reverse leakage current doubles for every 10 degree C rise.
- The impedance of a diode is approx = 25/I ohms (where I is the current in mA).

## Uses of a diode
### *Rectification*

### *Auctioning*

The output voltage Vout, is always the highest positive voltage between V1, V2 or V3. When V1, V2, and V3 are digital signals, the circuit operates as an OR gate where Vout is only a logic 1 when V1, V2 or V3 is logic 1.

### *Clamping*

IC1 is connected as a voltage follower. The IC may be damaged if the input voltage exceeds the +15V and -15V supply rails. To prevent this happening, D1 and D2 clamp the input voltage to the +15V rail and the -15V rail respectively. R1 limits the current during the clamping process.

### *Creating a voltage pedestal*

The forward drop of a diode is approximately 0.6V and may be considered constant for varying currents through it. The forward drop may be used as a crude 0.6V zener to create a voltage source or pedestal. In the circuit opposite, two diodes are used D1 and D2 to create a voltage for the time delay circuit R2 - C2. When the gate turn-off thyristor TH1 is triggered approximately 1.2V appears across D1 and D2. C2 charges via R2 and when the gate threshold voltage of TH2 is reached, TH2 is triggered and turns TH1 off by GTO action.

### Temperature compensation

The circuit diagram shows a class A-B push pull audio power amplifier. If D1 and D2 were not present there would be crossover distortion in the output stage TR1 and TR2 due to the fact that the base-emitter voltages of TR1 and TR2 have to be overcome before they can be turned on to supply current to the output. D1 and D2 cause TR1 and TR2 to be biased on slightly so that there is a small current flow through both devices from the positive rail to 0V. When a signal is being amplified, D1 and D2 thus ensure there is a smooth transition of conduction between TR1 and TR2. When TR1 and TR2 heat up however, their base-emitter voltage drops reduce which would lead to an increase in the current through them and a risk of overheating. If D1 and D2 are in thermal contact with TR1 and TR2 however, the forward drops in D1 and D2 will also reduce and tend to compensate for TR1 and TR2.

### Catching inductive current

When a transistor is used to energize a relay or solenoid, energy is stored in the magnetic field of the solenoid due to the current flowing through it. When the transistor is turned off, the inductive current must continue to flow. If D1 was not present, then the voltage at the collector of TR1 would rise until the transistor was destroyed. The inductive current would then flow through the destroyed transistor until all the energy in the coil was dissipated. D1 provides a path for the inductive current which circulates through the diode which clamps the collector voltage of the transistor to approximately 0.6V above the positive supply rail.

### Increasing the voltage withstand capability of another device.

The circuit opposite uses TR1 and TR2 as emitter followers to increase the current drive of the NAND gates so as to drive LED1. The reverse breakdown voltage of the base-emitter junction of most transistors is only a few volts. The NAND gates are powered from 15V, consequently, if the output of IC1/1 was at a logic 0 and IC1/2 at a logic 1, the base-emitter junction of TR1 would break down if D1 was not present.

## *DC restoration*

The square wave ac input to the above circuit has a peak to peak amplitude of 15V. It is required to drive a CMOS logic gate IC1/1 which is powered from a 15V rail. The input to the logic gate must ideally switch between 0V and +15V. If a diode is used to rectify the input waveform then the input to the logic gate would only switch from between approximately 0V and 7V. In the circuit above, C1 and D1 "pin" the input waveform's negative edge to the 0V rail so that almost the full 15V amplitude is now presented to the logic gate.

### ✍ Testing a diode

A silicon diode is best tested with an analogue multimeter (such as an AVO). The meter has an internal battery which applies voltage to the diode to test whether it will conduct or block current. The positive of the battery is actually connected to the negative lead of the meter. This is because current normally flows into the meter when it is used on the volts and current ranges. When the meter is used on the ohms range, current flows from the meter to the component being tested; the meter needle would move in the wrong direction if the meter's internal battery was not connected with its positive terminal to the negative lead of the battery. (On digital multimeters, the positive lead of the internal battery is connected to the positive lead of the meter).

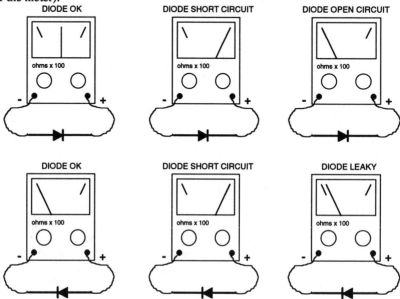

Ensure that fingers do not touch any of the leads.

## Common signal diodes

| TYPE No | TYPE | MANFR | $V_R$ max | $I_F$ (AV) | $I_F$ (DC) max | $I_{FRM}$ max | $I_{FSM}$ max | $I_R$ max @ 25 °C | $V_F$ max @ $I_F$ | $t_{rr}$ max | MAX DIMENSIONS |
|---|---|---|---|---|---|---|---|---|---|---|---|
| 1N914 | Switch | Philips | 75V | - | 75mA | 225mA | 0.5A, 1S | 5uA | 1V @ 10mA | 4nS | |
| 1N916 | Switch | Philips | 75V | - | 75mA | 225mA | 0.5A, 1S | 5uA | 1V @ 10mA | 4nS | |
| BAW62 | Logic | Philips | 75V | - | 200mA | 450mA | 2A, 1uS | 5uA | 1V@ 100mA | 4nS | |
| 1N4148 | Switch | Philips | 75V | - | 200mA | 450mA | 2A, 1uS | 25nA* | 1V @ 10mA | 4nS | |
| 1N4448 | Switch | Philips | 75V | - | 200mA | 450mA | 2A, 1uS | 25nA* | 1V @ 20mA | 4nS | |
| OA202 | Genpur | Philips | 150V | - | 160mA | 250mA | --- | 100nA | 1.15V@30mA | 3.5uS | |
| BY206 | Fast Recovery | Motorola | 350V | 0.6A | - | - | 25A | - | 1.2V @ 2A | 200nS | 3.05  6.6  0.86 |
| BA481 | Schottky-barrier | Philips | 4V | - | 30mA | - | - | 10uA | 0.6 @ 10mA | - | 1.7  2.6  0.55 DO34 |
| BAT85 | | Philips | 30V | - | 200mA | - | 600mA | 2uA | 0.4V @ 10mA | 5nS | |
| BYX10 | High Voltage | G.I. | 800V | 0.36 A | - | 15A | - | 1uA | 1.6V @ 2A | 2uStyp | 2.7  5.2  0.86 DO41 |

\* @100 DEGREES C

Source:- Motorola, Philips, GI

# Zener diodes

If a diode manufactured from heavily doped silicon is reverse biased, reverse conduction gradually starts to occur at around 6V. This is termed zener breakdown and is also seen on reverse biased base-emitter junctions of transistors. If the silicon is lightly doped however, reverse conduction occurs at a much higher reverse voltage and the effect happens more suddenly. This is termed avalanche breakdown.

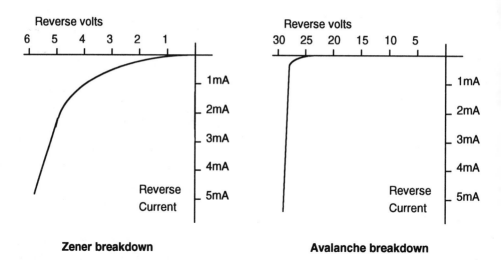

**Zener breakdown**　　　　　　　**Avalanche breakdown**

Diodes which are specifically manufactured to employ one of these effects are called zener diodes.

---

### ✋ Rules of thumb

- The current through a zener diode must be limited by the external circuit.
- Zeners below about 5.1V have a "soft" characteristic - zener breakdown.
- Zeners below about 5.1V have a negative temperature coefficient.
- Higher voltage zeners diodes have a sharper characteristic - avalanche breakdown.
- Zeners above about 5.1V have a positive temperature coefficient.
- Zeners around about 5.1V have almost  zero temperature coefficient.
- Zeners may also be used in the normal forward diode mode.

## Uses of a zener diode

### *Voltage regulation*

In the example opposite, a 15V dc regulated supply is produced from the 50V battery. When no load is connected to the 15V supply, all the current supplied via R1 flows through the zener. In this case it is (50 - 15)/1000 = 35mA. The zener diode must be capable of dissipating the power in this condition which is 0.525 watts. The 15V supply is only capable of supplying about 30mA after which the output voltage starts to fall.

### *Threshold device*

When power is first applied, the voltage across C1 ( and hence across ZD1) is zero and the zener diode cannot conduct. C1 charges up via R1 and when the voltage exceeds 15V, ZD1 starts to conduct, when there is sufficient current flowing through ZD1 and into the base of TR1, the transistor turns on and energizes the relay. The circuit thus provides a time delay for the turn on of a relay when power is first applied.

### *Voltage clamp*

Electronic circuits are sometimes required to operate in hazardous environments where explosive gases may be present. It is essential to limit the electrical power reaching those circuits to prevent ignition of the gas. The circuit opposite is referred to as a zener barrier; the zener diode ZD1 limits the maximum voltage to 10V. The current through the zener is limited by R1 and the current to the hazardous area is limited by R1 and R2.

---

### ✄ ✄ Testing a zener diode

Is the same procedure as testing a diode. See page 62.

## Zener diodes 500mW

| WATTAGE | TYPE No | RANGE | TOL AVAIL | Tj °C MAX | MANFR | | MAX DIMENSIONS |
|---|---|---|---|---|---|---|---|
| 500mW | BZV55 | 2V7 to 20V | ±2% to ±20% | 175°C | Thomson | | 1.7  3.04  0.55  DO34 |
| 500mW | BZV60 | 2V4 to 75V E24 | ±2%, ±5% | - | Philips | | 1.7  3.04  0.55  DO34 |
| 500mW | BZX55 | 0V8 to 62V / 2V4 to 91V | ±2%, ±5% | 175°C / 200°C | ITT / Thomson / Motorola | | 2.29  5.08  0.56  DO35 |
| 500mW | BZX79 | 2V4 to 75V / 2V4 to 200V | ±2%,±5% | 155°C | Philips / Motorola | | 2.29  5.08  0.56  DO35 |
| 500mW | BZX83 | 2V7 to 33V | ±5% | 175°C | Motorola | | 2.29  5.08  0.56  DO35 |
| 500mW | BZY88 | 2V7 to 33V | ±2%, ±5% | 200°C | Motorola | | 2.29  5.08  0.56  DO35 |
| 500mW | ZPD / M-ZPD | 1V to 51V / 3V9 to 100V | ±2%, ±5% | 175°C / 200°C | ITT / Motorola | ITT is DO35 outline | 2.71  5.2  0.86  DO41 |

**Zener diodes 1.3W**

| WATTAGE | TYPE No | RANGE | TOL AVAIL | Tj °C MAX | MANFR | $\theta_{junc\text{-}case}$ | MAX DIMENSIONS |
|---|---|---|---|---|---|---|---|
| 1.3W | BZD23 | 7V5 to 270 | ±5% | 200°C | Philips | - | 2.15, 4.3, 0.81 SOD81 |
| 1.3W | BZV85 | 3V6 to 75V | ±5% | 200°C | Philips | 110°C / W | 2.6, 4.8, 0.81 DO41 |
| 1.3W | BZX85 | 2V7 to 150 / 3V3 to 100 | ±2%,±5% | 175°C | ITT,Thomson / Motorola | 110°C / W | 2.71, 5.2, 0.86 DO41 |
| 1.3W | MZD | 3V9 to200V | ±1,2,5% | 200°C | Motorola | - | 2.71, 5.2, 0.86 DO41 |
| 1.3W | ZPY / M-ZPY | 3V9 to 100 | ±2%, ±5% | 200°C | Thomson / Motorola | 110°C / W | 2.71, 5.2, 0.86 DO41 |

**Zener diodes 1.5 to 2W**

| WATTAGE | TYPE No | RANGE | TOL AVAIL | Tj °C MAX | MANFR | $\theta$ junc-case | MAX DIMENSIONS |
|---------|---------|-------|-----------|-----------|-------|---------|----------------|
| 1.5W | BZY97 | 3V3 to 200<br>7V5 to 200 | ±5% | 150°C | Thomson<br>Fagor | 60°C / W | 3.05 6.35 0.86 **F126** |
| 1.5W | ZGP10 | 100 to 200V | ±5,10,20% | 175°C | G.I. | -°C / W | 2.71 5.2 0.86 **DO41** |

# Bipolar transistors

NPN     PNP     TO-18     TO-39     TO-3

TO-92   TO-126     TO-202     TO-220   TO-218

The bipolar transistor is a current-operated amplifying device. When a current is injected into the base with respect to the emitter, a much larger current is caused to flow between the collector and the emitter and may be in the order of 100 times the magnitude of the base current. Although the collector to emitter current is slightly affected by the voltage applied between the collector and the emitter, the current may be considered a current source which is controlled by the base current.

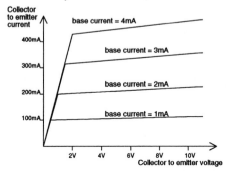

The curves opposite show the collect to emitter current for a typical NPN transistor for four different values of injected base current. When 1 mA is injected into the base with respect to the emitter, then provided the voltage between the collector and the emitter is greater than approximately 0.5V, 100mA is caused to flow between the collector and the emitter. As the collector to emitter voltage is increased, the collector to emitter current is also increased slightly and this is shown by the curve of "base current = 1mA" not being parallel to the x axis.

## 👍 Rules of thumb

- The base current flows iN on an NPN (out on a PNP).
- When current is injected into the base a voltage drop of approx 0.6V is created between the base and emitter.
- This voltage drop reduces by 2.5mV for every degree C rise in temperature.
- A reverse biased base-emitter junction zeners at about 5V.
- The collector to emitter voltage saturation voltage is approximately 0.3V for a signal transistor. It may be a volt or more for a power transistor.
- The current gain between the base-emitter and the collector-emitter increases with increase in temperature.
- The collector-emitter leakage current doubles for every 10 degree C rise in temperature.

## Uses of a transistor

### *Common-emitter voltage amplifier*

Although the bipolar transistor is a current amplifying device, it may be configured as a voltage amplifier by using a resistor (R1) to convert the input voltage signal to a current suitable for driving the base and using a resistor (R2) to convert the collector current of the transistor to an output voltage. The input signal voltage must be greater than the base-emitter voltage of 0.6V however. There is an inversion from input to output in that the output voltage measured with respect to 0V, falls as the input voltage rises.

### *Current source*

The base of TR1 is set at 5.6V below the 18V rail by ZD1. Consequently the emitter is set at approximately 5V below the 18V rail. A current of 5mA therefore flows through R2. Most of this current continues to flow out of the collector of TR1 and the collector constitutes a constant current source which may drive a load of between a short circuit and 10k without the current being significantly affected.

### *Transistor switch*

A transistor may be used as a switch having only two possible states; on or off. It may be used to turn on a lamp or other device in response to a signal applied to the base of the transistor. In the circuit opposite, a 12V lamp is being controlled by TR1. When a dc signal is applied to the input, TR1 is turned on by the base current derived by R1. The value of R1 must be such that the base current times the current gain of TR1 exceeds the current rating of the lamp. This ensures that TR1 saturates i.e. the collector-emitter voltage is almost zero. The lamp then receives its rated voltage. When the input signal is removed, the transistor turns off and the lamp is extinguished. R2 ensures the transistor cannot be turned partially on by providing an alternative path for the collector-base leakage current.

## Testing a transistor

Is a similar process to testing a diode. See page 63. The transistor may be considered to be two series connected diodes which have their anodes commoned at the base terminal for an NPN transistor (the cathodes are commoned at the base for a PNP transistor).

It is a good idea to familarise yourself with the readings of a known good transistor and make a mark on the meter's scale with a felt-tip pen as a reference. The forward biased junctions of a power transistor give a greater deflection than a signal transistor.

All three combinations of leads must be tested, i.e. collector-base, emitter-base, and collector-emitter. The above procedure is repeated for the emitter-base junction. The collector-emitter test should give no deflection in either direction (even with the meter set to ohms x 10k) unless the transistor is a special type with an integral collector to emitter diode e.g. a television line-output transistor. Care must be taken not to touch the test leads as leakage through the body can be mistaken for a leaky junction. Testing of a PNP transistor is simply the inverse of the procedure detailed above; (swap the meter leads).

## Bipolar transistor parameter definitions
### *Ic cont (maximum)*
The maximum continuous dc collector current which may be drawn, provided:
1. due regard is given to the safe operating area curve published by the transistor manufacturer,
2. the transistor is not made to dissipate power which would cause the junction temperature to exceed Tj.

### $V_{CE0}$
The maximum allowable collector to emitter voltage with the base terminal left open circuit. This is generally the worst case condition such that all other operating modes will be safe if the designer does not allow the collector to emitter voltage to exceed this value.

### $P_{tot}$ *(max)*

TRANSISTOR MOUNTING BASE TEMPERATURE

Ptot is the maximum allowable power dissipation (in watts) when the mounting base of the transistor is at 25°C . This is very rarely achievable, and the maximum allowable power of the transistor must be derated for mounting base temperatures of greater than 25°C according to a de-rating chart. A typical chart is shown opposite.

### $H_{FE}$ *(min)* @ $I_C$
Is the ratio of dc collector current to dc base current at the stated collector current. The figure given is the guaranteed minimum value at 25 degrees C. $H_{FE}$ increases in value as temperature increases, and reduces in value as collector current increases.

### *Tj °C*
Is the maximum allowable junction temperature in degrees C (see Ptot above).

### *ICEO max*
Is the collector cut-off current with the base open circuit. It is a measure of the maximum leakage current which would flow when the collector-base junction is reverse biased (which is the normal condition). It is given at 25 degrees C. It tends to double in value for every 10 degrees C increase in temperature.

### $f_T$ *(min)*
Is called the transition frequency. It is the frequency at which the small signal gain of the transistor tends to extrapolate to unity. It is a measure of the transistor's high frequency performance.

### *°C/W junc - case*
Is the thermal impedance of the transistor and represents the rise in temperature (for each watt of power dissipated) of the transistor's chip above the temperature of the transistor's metal mounting surface. It is used to calculate the chip temperaure when the transistor is mounted on a heat sink.

Common TO92 transistors

| OUTLINE | NPN | PNP | MANFR | APPL | VCEO | Ic max | P tot @25°C | hFE min @ Ic | Tj °C | ICBO max @ 25 °C | fT (typ) | °C /W Junc-amb |
|---|---|---|---|---|---|---|---|---|---|---|---|---|
| TO92 | BC237 |  | Motorola | Amplifier | 45V | 0.1A | 0.35W | 120 @ 2mA | 150°C | 15nA | 100MHz | 357 |
|  |  | BC307 | Philips |  | -45V | -0.1A | 0.5W | 120 @ 2mA |  |  | 300MHz | 250 |
|  | BC546 |  |  |  | 65V | 0.1A |  | 110 @ 2mA |  |  |  |  |
|  |  | BC556 |  |  | -65V | -0.1A |  | 75 @ 2mA |  |  |  |  |
|  | BC547 |  |  |  | 45V | 0.1A |  | 110 @ 2mA |  |  |  |  |
|  |  | BC557 |  |  | -45V | -0.1A |  | 75 @ 2mA |  |  |  |  |
|  | BC548 |  |  | Low-noise | 30V | 0.1A |  | 110 @ 2mA |  |  |  |  |
|  |  | BC558 |  |  | -30V | -0.1A |  | 75 @ 2mA |  |  |  |  |
|  | BC549 |  |  | Audio | 30V | 0.1A |  | 125 @2mA |  |  |  |  |
|  |  | BC559 |  | driver | -30V | -0.1A |  | 125 @2mA |  | 100nA | 200MHz | 200 |
|  | BC337 |  |  |  | 45V | 0.5A | 0.8W | 100 @ 0.1A |  |  |  |  |
|  |  | BC327 |  |  | -45V | -0.5A |  | 100 @ 0.1A |  |  |  |  |
| TO92 | 2N3903 |  | Philips | Switching | 40V | 0.2A | 0.625W | 50 @ 10mA | 150°C |  | 250MHz | 357 |
|  |  | 2N3905 |  |  | -40V | -0.2A |  | 50 @ 10mA |  |  | 200MHz | 357 |
|  | MPSA43 |  |  |  | 65V | 0.1A |  | 100 @ 10mA |  |  | 300MHz | 357 |
|  |  | 2N3906 |  |  | -65V | -0.1A |  | 100 @ 10mA |  |  | 250MHz | 357 |
|  | MPSA42 |  |  | High voltage | 200V | 0.5A |  | 40 @ 10mA |  |  | 50MHz | 200 |
|  |  | MPSA93 |  |  | -200V | -0.5A |  | 40 @ 10mA |  |  | 50MHz | 200 |
|  |  |  |  |  | 300V | 0.5A |  | 40 @ 10mA |  |  | 50MHz | 200 |
|  |  | MPSA92 |  |  | -300V | -0.5A |  | 40 @ 10mA |  |  | 50MHz | 200 |

**Common TO92 transistors - continued**

| OUTLINE | NPN | PNP | MANFR | APPL | VCEO | Ic max | P tot @25°C | hFE min @ Ic | Tj °C | ICBO max @ 25 °C | fT (typ) | °C /W Junc-amb |
|---|---|---|---|---|---|---|---|---|---|---|---|---|
| TO92 | BC182L | | Motorola | General | 50V | 0.1A | 0.35W | 100 @ 2mA | 150°C | 15nA | 150MHz | 357 |
| | | BC212L | | purpose | -50V | -0.1A | | 60 @ 2mA | | | | |
| | BC183L | | Philips | | 30V | 0.1A | | 100 @ 2mA | | | | |
| | | BC213L | | | -30V | -0.1A | | 80 @ 2mA | | | | |
| | BC184L | | | Low | 30V | 0.1A | | 250 @ 2mA | | | | |
| | | BC214L | | noise | -30V | -0.1A | | 140 @ 2mA | | | | |
| | 2N3704 | | | General | 30V | 0.8A | 0.625 | 100 @50mA | | | | |
| | | 2N3702 | | purpose | -25V | -0.2A | W | 100 @50mA | | | | |
| | 2N3705 | | | | 30V | 0.8A | | 250 @2mA | | | | |
| | | 2N3703 | | | -30V | -0.1A | | 140 @2mA | | | | |
| | TIPP31 | | | Power | 30V | 2A | 0.8W | 20 @ 1A | | | | |
| | | TIPP32 | | switching | -30V | -2A | 1.25W | 25 @ 1A | | | | |
| | TIPP31A | | | | 60V | 2A | 0.8W | 20 @ 1A | | | | |
| | | TIPP32A | | | -60V | -2A | 1.25W | 25 @ 1A | | | | |
| | TIPP31B | | | | 80V | 2A | 0.8W | 20 @ 1A | | | | |
| | | TIPP32B | | | -80V | -2A | 1.25W | 25 @ 1A | | | | |
| | TIPP31C | | | | 100V | 2A | 0.8W | 20 @ 1A | | | | |
| | | TIPP32C | | | -100V | -2A | 1.25W | 25 @ 1A | | | | |
| | BC639 | | | Audio | 80V | 1A | 1W | 40 @ 0.15A | | 100nA | 130MHz | 156 |
| | | BC640 | | drivers | -80V | -1A | 1W | 40 @ 0.15A | | | 50MHz | 156 |

Source: Motorola, Philips

# Common TO39 transistors

| OUTLINE | NPN | PNP | MANFR | APPL | $V_{CEO}$ | Ic max | P tot @25°C | $h_{FE}$ min @ Ic | Tj °C | ICBO max @ 25°C | $f_T$ (typ) | °C/W Junc-case |
|---|---|---|---|---|---|---|---|---|---|---|---|---|
| TO39 | BFY51 | | Philips | Gen Pur | 30V | 1A | 0.8W | 40 @0.15A | 200°C | 500nA | 50MHz | 35 |
| | BFY50 | | Philips | Gen Pur | 35V | 1A | 0.8W | 30 @0.15A | 200°C | 500nA | 60MHz | 35 |
| | 2N2219 | | Philips | Switch | 30V | 0.8A | 0.8W | 75 @10mA | 200°C | 10nA | 250MHz | 50 |
| | | 2N2905 | Philips | Switch | -40V | -0.6A | 0.6W | 100 @0.15A | 200°C | 20nA | 200MHz | 58 |
| | 2N3053 | | Harris | Amp | 40V | 0.7A | 5W | 50 @0.15A | 200°C | 250nA | 100MHz | 35 |
| | | 2N4037 | Philips | Gen Pur | -40V | -1A | 7W | 50 @0.15A | 200°C | 250nA | 60MHz | 58.3 |
| | 2N1711 | | Philips | Amp | 50V | 1A | 0.8W | 100 @0.15A | 200°C | 10nA | 70MHz | 25 |
| | | 2N4036 | Philips | Amp | -65V | -1A | 7W | 20 @0.15A | 175°C | 20nA | ? | 25 |
| | BC301 | | Thomson | ? | 60V | 1A | 0.85W | 40 @0.15A | 175°C | ? | 60MHz | ? |
| | BFX85 | | Philips | Gen Pur | 60V | 1A | 0.8W | 70 @0.15A | 200°C | 500nA | 50MHz | 35 |
| | 2N3019 | | Philips | Amp | 80V | 1A | 0.8W | 100 @0.15A | 200°C | 10nA | 100MHz | 35 |
| | 2N3440 | | Philips | Switch | 250V | 1A | 1W | 40 @20mA | 200°C | 100nA | 70MHz | 58.3 |
| | | 2N5415 | Philips | Switch | -200V | -1A | 1W | 30 @50mA | 200°C | 50uA | 15MHz | 17.5 |
| | 2N3439 | | Philips | Switch | 350V | 1A | 1W | 30 @2mA | 200°C | 100nA | 70MHz | 58.3 |
| | | 2N5416 | Philips | Switch | -300V | -1A | 1W | 30 @50mA | 200°C | 50uA | 15MHz | 17.5 |

Source:- Philips, Harris, Thomson

1A - TO220 power transistors

| OUTLINE | NPN | PNP | MANFR | APPL | Ic cont | VCEO | P tot @25°C | hFE min @ Ic | Tj °C | ICEO max @ 25°C | fT (min) | °C /W Junc-case |
|---|---|---|---|---|---|---|---|---|---|---|---|---|
| TO220 | TIP29A | | Motorola | Gen pur | 1A | 60V | 30W | 15 @1A | 150°C | 0.3mA | 3MHz | 4.167 |
| | | TIP30A | | Gen pur | 1A | -60V | 30W | 15 @1A | | 0.3mA | 3MHz | 4.167 |
| | TIP29B | | | Gen pur | 1A | 80V | 30W | 15 @1A | | 0.3mA | 3MHz | 4.167 |
| | | TIP30B | | Gen pur | 1A | -80V | 30W | 15 @1A | | 0.3mA | 3MHz | 4.167 |
| | TIP29C | | | Gen pur | 1A | 100V | 30W | 15 @1A | | 0.3mA | 3MHz | 4.167 |
| | | TIP30C | | Gen pur | 1A | -100V | 30W | 15 @1A | | 0.3mA | 3MHz | 4.167 |
| | TIP47 | | | Audio & switchg | 1A | 250V | 40W | 10 @1A | | 1mA | 10MHz | 3.125 |
| | TIP48 | MJE5730 | | | 1A | 300V | 40W | 10 @1A | | 1mA | 10MHz | 3.125 |
| | | | | | 1A | -300V | 40W | 10 @1A | | 1mA | 10MHz | 3.125 |
| | TIP49 | MJE5731 | | | 1A | 350V | 40W | 10 @1A | | 1mA | 10MHz | 3.125 |
| | | | | | 1A | -350V | 40W | 10 @1A | | 1mA | 10MHz | 3.125 |
| | TIP50 | MJE5732 | | | 1A | 400V | 40W | 10 @1A | | 1mA | 10MHz | 3.125 |
| | | | | | 1A | -400V | 40W | 10 @1A | | 1mA | 10MHz | 3.125 |

Source:- Motorola

## 2 to 3A - TO220 power transistors

| OUTLINE | NPN | PNP | MANFR | APPL | Ic cont | VCEO | P tot @25°C | hFE min @ Ic | Tj °C | ICEO max @ 25°C | fT (min) | °C /W Junc-case |
|---|---|---|---|---|---|---|---|---|---|---|---|---|
| TO220 | BD239A | | Motorola | Gen pur | 2A | 60V | 30W | 15 @ 1A | 150°C | 0.3mA | 3MHz | 4.167 |
| | | BD240A | | | -2A | -60V | 30W | 15 @ 1A | | 0.3mA | 3MHz | 4.167 |
| | BD239B | | | | 2A | 80V | 30W | 15 @ 1A | | 0.3mA | 3MHz | 4.167 |
| | | BD240B | | | -2A | -80V | 30W | 15 @ 1A | | 0.3mA | 3MHz | 4.167 |
| | BD239C | | | | 2A | 100V | 30W | 15 @ 1A | | 0.3mA | 3MHz | 4.167 |
| | | BD240C | | | -2A | -100V | 30W | 15 @ 1A | | 0.3mA | 3MHz | 4.167 |
| | BUX84 | | | SMPS | 2A | 400V | 50W | 30 @ 0.1A | | 0.2mA Ices | 4MHz | 2.5 |
| | BUX85 | | | SMPS | 2A | 450V | 50W | 30 @ 0.1A | | 0.2mA Ices | 4MHz | 2.5 |
| | BU505 | | Philips | Deflecn | 2.5A | 700V | 75W | 2.2 @ 2A | | - | - | - |
| | TIP31A | | Motorola | Gen pur | 3A | 60V | 40W | 10 @ 3A | | 0.3mA | 3MHz | 3.125 |
| | | TIP32A | | | -3A | -60V | 40W | 10 @ 3A | | 0.3mA | 3MHz | 3.125 |
| | TIP31B | | | | 3A | 80V | 40W | 10 @ 3A | | 0.3mA | 3MHz | 3.125 |
| | | TIP32B | | | -3A | -80V | 40W | 10 @ 3A | | 0.3mA | 3MHz | 3.125 |
| | TIP31C | | | | 3A | 100V | 40W | 10 @ 3A | | 0.3mA | 3MHz | 3.125 |
| | | TIP32C | | | -3A | -100V | 40W | 10 @ 3A | | 0.3mA | 3MHz | 3.125 |

Source:- Motorola & Philips

**4 to 5A - TO220 power transistors**

| OUTLINE | NPN | PNP | MANFR | APPL | Ic cont | VCEO | P tot @25°C | hFE min @ Ic | Tj °C | ICEO max @ 25°C | fT (min) | °C /W Junc-case |
|---|---|---|---|---|---|---|---|---|---|---|---|---|
| TO220 | BD535 | BD536 | Motorola | Gen pur | 4A | 60V | 50W | 25 @ 2A | 150 | Ices 0.1mA | 3MHz | 2.5 |
| | D44C10 | D45C10 | | | -4A | -60V | 50W | 25 @ 2A | | 0.1mA | 3MHz | 2.5 |
| | | | | Switchg | 4A | 80V | 30W | 10 @ 2A | | 0.01mA | 50 typ | 4.2 |
| | | | | | -4A | -80V | 30W | 10 @ 2A | | 0.01mA | 40 typ | 4.2 |
| | BUL52B | | Semilab | SMPS | 4A | 400V | | | | | | |
| | MJE13004 | | Motorola | SMPS | 4A | 300V | 75W | 8 @ 2A | | Icev 1mA | 4MHz | 1.67 |
| | MJE13005 | | | | -4A | 400V | 75W | 8 @ 2A | | 1mA | 4MHz | 1.67 |
| | BUT11 | | Thomson | High voltage switch | 5A | 400V | 83W | - | | Ices 1mA Icer | - | 1.5 |
| | BUV46 | | Thomson | | 5A | 400V | 70W | - | | 0.1mA | - | 1.76 |

Source:- Motorola & Thomson

# 6 to 7A - TO220 power transistors

| OUTLINE | NPN | PNP | MANFR | APPL | Ic cont | VCEO | P tot @25°C | hFE min @ Ic | Tj °C | ICEO max @ 25°C | fT (min) | °C /W Junc-case |
|---|---|---|---|---|---|---|---|---|---|---|---|---|
| TO220 | TIP41A | | Motorola | Gen pur | 6A | 60V | 65W | 15 @ 3A | 150 | 0.7mA | 3MHz | 1.92 |
| | | TIP42A | | | -6A | -60V | 65W | 15 @ 3A | | 0.7mA | 3MHz | 1.92 |
| | TIP41B | | | | 6A | 80V | 65W | 15 @ 3A | | 0.7mA | 3MHz | 1.92 |
| | | TIP42B | | | -6A | -80V | 65W | 15 @ 3A | | 0.7mA | 3MHz | 1.92 |
| | TIP41C | | | | 6A | 100V | 65W | 15 @ 3A | | 0.7mA | 3MHz | 1.92 |
| | | TIP42C | | | -6A | -100V | 65W | 15 @ 3A | | 0.7mA | 3MHz | 1.92 |
| | BD243A | | | | 6A | 60V | 65W | 15 @ 3A | | 0.7mA | 3MHz | 1.92 |
| | | BD244A | | | -6A | -60V | 65W | 15 @ 3A | | 0.7mA | 3MHz | 1.92 |
| | BD243B | | | | 6A | 80V | 65W | 15 @ 3A | | 0.7mA | 3MHz | 1.92 |
| | | BD244B | | | -6A | -80V | 65W | 15 @ 3A | | 0.7mA | 3MHz | 1.92 |
| | BD243C | | | | 6A | 100V | 65W | 15 @ 3A | | 0.7mA | 3MHz | 1.92 |
| | | BD244C | | | -6A | -100V | 65W | 15 @ 3A | | 0.7mA | 3MHz | 1.92 |
| | 2N6292 | | | | 7A | 70V | 40W | 30 @ 2A | | 1mA | 4MHz | 3.125 |
| | | 2N6107 | | | -7A | -70V | 40W | 30 @ 2A | | 1mA | 10MHz | 3.125 |
| | BU407 | | | Deflec | 7A | 150V | 60W | 30 @ 1.5A | | Ices 5mA | 10MHz | 2.08 |
| | BU406 | | | | 7A | 200V | 60W | 30 @ 1.5A | | 5mA | 10MHz | 2.08 |

b c e

Source:- Motorola

79

Common TO3 power transistors

| OUTLINE | NPN | PNP | MANFR | APPL | V$_{CEO}$ | Ic max | P tot @25°C | hFE min @ Ic | Tj °C | ICEO max @ 25°C | f$_T$ (min) | °C /W Junc-case |
|---|---|---|---|---|---|---|---|---|---|---|---|---|
| TO3 | 2N3771 | | Motorola | Linear | 40V | 30A | 150W | 15 @15A | 200°C | 10mA | 0.2MHz | 1.17 |
| | 2N3055 | MJ2955 | | Gen pur | 60V | 15A | 115W | 20 @ 4A | 200°C | 0.7mA | 2.5MHz | 1.52 |
| | | | | Gen pur | -60V | -15A | 115W | 20 @ 4A | 200°C | 0.7mA | 2.5MHz | 1.52 |
| | 2N3772 | | | Linear | 60V | 20A | 150W | 15 @10A | 200°C | 10mA | 0.2MHz | 1.17 |
| | 2N3716 | | | Amp | 80V | 10A | 150W | 50 @ 1A | 200°C | - | - | 1.17 |
| | | 2N3792 | | Amp | -80V | -10A | 150W | 50 @ 1A | 200°C | - | - | 1.17 |
| | MJ802 | | | Audio | 90V | 30A | 200W | 25 @ 7.5A | 200°C | Icbo 1mA | 2MHz | 0.875 |
| | 2N3773 | | | Audio | 140V | 16A | 150W | 15 @ 8A | 200°C | 10mA | - | 1.17 |
| | | 2N6609 | | Audio | -140V | -16A | 150W | 15 @ 8A | 200°C | 10mA | - | 1.17 |
| | MJ15003 | | | Audio | 140V | 20A | 250W | 25 @ 5A | 200°C | 10mA | 2MHz | 0.7 |
| | | MJ15004 | | Audio | 140V | 20A | 250W | 25 @ 5A | 200°C | 0.25mA | 2MHz | 0.7 |
| | BUX48A | | | SMPS | 450V | 15A | 175W | 8 @ 8A | 200°C | 0.25mA | - | 1 |
| | MJ16002A | | | SMPS | 500V | 5A | 125W | 5 @ 5A | 200°C | - | - | 1.4 |
| | MJ16006 | | | | 450V | 8A | 150W | 5 @ 8A | 200°C | - | - | 1.17 |
| | MJ16010 | | | | 450V | 15A | 175W | 5 @ 15A | 200°C | - | - | 1 |
| | BU208A | | | TV | 700V | 5A | 12.5W | 2.25 @ 4.5A | 200°C | - | 4MHz typ | 1.6 |

case is collector

pin view

Source:- Motorola

# Triacs

MAIN TERMINAL 2

GATE | MAIN TERMINAL 1

MT1 G MT2

MT1 MT2 G

TAB MAY BE MT2
OR ISOLATED

The triac is a semiconductor switch device which can control ac power. It is effectively two thyristors back to back with a common gate terminal. Before it is triggered, the triac will block current in either direction. It may be triggered into conduction by positive or negative gate current and current may then flow in either direction between main terminals 1 and 2. Once the device is triggered, the gate signal may be removed and conduction will continue until the main terminal current falls below the holding current at which point the device reverts to the blocking condition. There are four possible operating modes: (triggering is always with respect to MT1)

MT2 +VE

QUADRANT 2 (I-)
+ve main current
-ve Gate current

QUADRANT I (I+)
+ve main current
+ve Gate current

GATE +VE

QUADRANT 3 (III-)
-ve main current
-ve Gate current

QUADRANT 4 (III+)
-ve main current
+ve Gate current

## 👍 Rules of thumb

- The gate current is always derived with respect to MT1 (this may be thought of as the cathode).
- Quadrant 4 is usually less sensitive to triggering than the other 3.
- When gate current is derived from MT2, the triac is operating in quadrants 1 and 3 only.
- Always use a gate to MT1 resistor to assist turn-off and reduce false triggering ( 1k).

## Uses of a triac
### *Electronic switch*

The triac may be used to switch a load such as an incandescent lamp on an ac supply. The triac is always triggered with respect to the main terminal 1 and in the circuit opposite the trigger signal may be a positive or a negative dc voltage or an ac voltage.

### *Lamp dimmer*

The triggering signal for the triac is derived from its main terminal 2 (MT2) VR1 and C1 provide a delay in triggering

## Triac voltage rating letter codes

Some manufacturers such as Philips signify the voltage rating of a triac device by a numbered suffix actually detailing the maximum voltage e.g. BT136-600 is a 600V device. Many manufacturers use the following suffix letter code convention:-

| SUFFIX LETTER | VOLTAGE RATING | SUFFIX LETTER | VOLTAGE RATING |
|---|---|---|---|
| Y | 30V | M | 600V |
| F | 60V | S | 700V |
| A | 100V | N | 800V |
| B | 200V | P | 1000V |
| C | 300V | V | 1200V |
| D | 400V | Z | 1400V |

## ✎✎ Testing a triac

Testing a triac is a similar process to testing a transistor; see page 73. The MT1 to gate test gives a reading similar to a forward biased P-N junction but a greater deflection and the same in either direction. A test should be conducted with a known good triac so that the normal deflection may be recorded. The MT1-MT2 test should show no deflection in either direction, however there will be no difference between a normal reading and an open circuit triac. The final test must be made with the device connected into the equipment.

Ensure that fingers do not touch any of the leads.

Common TO220 isolated triacs

| OUTLINE | TYPE No | MANFR | $I_T$ (RMS) | $I_{TSM}$ | $V_{DRM}$ | dv/dt | dv/dt$_c$ | $V_{GT}$ | $I^2t$ | di/dt | $I_{GT}$ MT2+ G+ | MT2+ G- | MT2- G- | MT2- G+ | Tj °C | °C /W Junc-case |
|---|---|---|---|---|---|---|---|---|---|---|---|---|---|---|---|---|
| TO220 tab is isolated | BT136F-600 | Philips | 4A | 25A | 600V | 100V/uS | 10V/uS | 1.5V | 4A²s | 10A/uS | 35mA | 35mA | 35mA | 70mA | 110 | - |
| | T0409MJ | TAG | 4A | 35A | 600V | 50V/uS | 2V/uS | 2.5V | 6.1A²s | - | 10mA | 10mA | 10mA | 10mA | 125 | 5.75 |
| | BTA06-600BW | Thomson | 6A | 60A | 600V | 500V/uS | - | 1.5V | 18A²s | 20A/uS | 50mA | 50mA | 50mA | - | 125 | 4.3 |
| | T0609MJ | TAG | 6A | 55A | 600V | 50V/uS | 2V/uS | 2.5V | 15A²s | - | 10mA | 10mA | 10mA | 10mA | 125 | 4.75 |
| | BTA08-600BW | Thomson | 8A | 80A | 600V | 500V/uS | - | 1.5V | 32A²s | 20A/uS | 50mA | 50mA | 50mA | - | 125 | 4.3 |
| | T0810MJ | TAG | 8A | 100A | 600V | 200V/uS | 2V/uS | 2.5V | 50A²s | - | 25mA | 25mA | 25mA | 25mA | 125 | 3.4 |
| | BT137F-600 | Philips | 8A | 55A | 600V | 100V/uS | 10V/uS | 1.5V | 15A²s | 20A/uS | 35mA | 35mA | 35mA | 70mA | 110 | - |
| | T1010MJ | TAG | 10A | 110A | 600V | 200V/uS | 2V/uS | 2.5V | 60A²s | - | 25mA | 25mA | 25mA | 25mA | 125 | 3.4 |
| MT2 G / MT1 | BT138F-600 | Philips | 12A | 90A | 600V | 100V/uS | 10V/uS | 1.5V | 40A²s | 30A/uS | 35mA | 35mA | 35mA | 70mA | 110 | 5.5 |
| Philips devices are a SOT186 package | BTA12-600BW | Thomson | 12A | 120A | 600V | 500V/uS | - | 1.5V | 72A²s | 20A/uS | 50mA | 50mA | 50mA | - | 125 | 3.3 |
| | T1212MJ | TAG | 12A | 120A | 600V | 500V/uS | 5V/uS | 2.5V | 72A²s | - | 50mA | 50mA | 50mA | 50mA | 125 | 2.8 |

Source:- Philips, TAG, SGS-Thomson

In general: Suffix B=200V, D=400V, M=600V, N=800V

Common TO220 non-isolated triacs

| OUTLINE | TYPE No | MANFR | I_T (RMS) | I TSM | V_DRM | dv/dt | dv/dt c | V_GT | I_GT MT2+ G+ | MT2+ G- | MT2- G- | MT2- G+ | Tj °C | °C/W Junc-case |
|---|---|---|---|---|---|---|---|---|---|---|---|---|---|---|
| TO220 tab is MT2 | BT136-600 | Philips | 4A | 25A | 600V | 100V/uS | 10V/uS | 1.5V | 35mA | 35mA | 35mA | 70mA | 125°C | 3.7°C/W |
| | TIC206D | Texas | 4A | 30A | 400V | - | - | - | 5mA | 5mA | 5mA | 5mA | | |
| | T0505MH | TAG | 5A | 40A | 600V | 10V/uS | 1V/uS | 2.5V | | | | | | 4°C/W |
| | BTB06-400BW | Thomson | 6A | 60A | 400V | - | - | - | 50mA | 50mA | 50mA | 50mA | | - |
| | TIC216M | Texas | 6A | 80A | 600V | - | - | - | | | | | | - |
| | BT137-600 | Philips | 8A | 55A | 600V | 100V/uS | 10V/uS | 1.5V | 35mA | 35mA | 35mA | 70mA | | 2.4°C/W |
| | T0805MH | TAG | 8A | 70A | 600V | 10V/uS | 1V/uS | 2.5V | 5mA | 5mA | 5mA | 5mA | | 3°C/W |
| | TIC225M | Texas | 8A | 80A | 600V | - | - | 2V | 5mA | 20mA | 10mA | 30mA | | - |
| | TIC226M | Texas | 8A | 80A | 600V | - | - | 2V | 50mA | 50mA | 50mA | 20mA | | - |
| | BTB08-600BW | Thomson | 8A | 80A | 600V | 500V/uS | 7V/uS | 1.5V | 50mA | 50mA | 50mA | - | | 3.5°C/W |
| | T1010MH | TAG | 10A | 100A | 600V | 200V/uS | 2V/uS | 2.5 | 50mA | 50mA | 50mA | 50mA | | 2.5°C/W |
| | BT138-600 | Philips | 12A | 90A | 600V | 100V/uS | 10V/uS | 1.5V | 35mA | 35mA | 35mA | 70mA | | 2°C/W |
| | TIC236M | Texas | 12A | 100A | 600V | - | - | 2V | 50mA | 50mA | 50mA | - | | - |
| | BTB12-600BW | Thomson | 12A | 120A | 600V | 500V/uS | 12V/uS | 1.5V | 50mA | 50mA | 50mA | - | | 2.7°C/W |

MT1   MT2   G

In general: Suffix B=200V, D=400V, M=600V, N=800V

Source:- Philips, TAG, Texas, SGS-Thomson

85

# Operational amplifiers

**SINGLE OP-AMP**

**DUAL OP-AMP**

**QUAD OP-AMP**

An operational amplifier (op-amp) is a high-gain differential amplifier which is capable of amplifying from dc up to frequencies in the order of 100kHz to 1 MHz depending upon the type used. It has a single-ended output i.e. the output is a voltage with respect to 0V of the power supply. There are two inputs however, one marked + and one marked - , and the op amp is designed to amplify the voltage difference between them. When the + input is made more positive than the - input, the output goes positive with respect to 0V.

Most op-amps require positive and negative power rails typically +15V and - 15V dc.

## ✥ Rules of thumb

- The op-amp has very high gain, very high input impedance, and very low output impedance.
- The output gives a voltage (with respect to 0V) which is proportional to the difference in voltage between the two inputs; when the positive input is more positive than the negative input, the output voltage will be positive with respect to 0V.
- A dual rail op-amp can only operate correctly if the input signals are within approximately 3V of the power supply rails.
- A dual rail op-amp can only give an output voltage to within approximately 3V of the power supply rails.
- The impedance levels at the two inputs should be made the same to reduce input offset current effects.

# Op-amp parameters

## *Supply voltage rails*
Most op-amps are designed to operate from positive and negative dc supply rails. Typically these are +15V and - 15V. The op-amp parameters will be specified at the nominal power supply rails. Most manufacturers specify absolute maximum supply rails of typically 3V above the nominal.

## *Supply quiescent current*
The total current an op-amp will draw from both supply rails (at their nominal value) when no load is connected to the output.

## *Input offset voltage (Vos)*
If the difference between the two inputs is made equal to zero, in practice the output voltage will not be zero due to slight manufacturing differences in the transistors. A very small voltage difference must be applied to the inputs to make the output zero. This input voltage is termed the input offset voltage.

## *Input offset voltage drift*
The above parameter will drift with changes in temperature. Manufacturers quote a typical figure in microvolts per degree C.

## *Common-mode input voltage range (CM range)*
In most applications of op-amps, the two input voltages are almost the same, however they must not be allowed to fall outside of the common mode input voltage range otherwise the op-amp may not operate correctly or at worst be permanently damaged.

### Differential-mode input voltage range (DM range)
In most op-amp applications, the two inputs are within a few millivolts of each other. Some applications such as comparators may call for the two inputs to be different by several volts. The design of the op-amp may not allow this because of input protection diodes or the design of the input transistor stages. The DM range specifies the maximum allowable voltage difference between the two inputs.

### Common-mode rejection ratio CMRR
Specifies how good an op-amp is at rejecting (not amplifying) signals that are present at both inputs simultaneously. The CMRR is the ratio of the common mode input voltage to the output voltage which is due to the common mode voltage. It is specified in decibels. (20 Log V ratio).

### Input bias current
The input transistors of the op-amp require small constant currents so that they can operate correctly and these currents usually flow into the amplifier input terminals. They are termed Input Bias Currents $I_{ib+}$ and $I_{ib-}$ and are specified with the output voltage = 0. Ideally these currents should be equal, however, in practice they are different and the difference is termed input offset current. Data sheets specify the average of the two input bias currents.

### Input offset current
The difference between $I_{ib+}$ and $I_{ib-}$ when the output voltage is zero.

### Input resistance
Is the resistance measured at one input when the other input is connected to 0V.

### Slew rate
Is the maximum rate of change of voltage the output can achieve when the op-amp has feedback connected and a step change in input voltage is applied. The slew rate limits the sine-wave frequency at which an op-amp can amplify and give the highest peak-to-peak output voltage without distortion. Slew rate is specified in volts per microsecond. An amplifier which is showing slew rate limitations is seen to give a triangular-wave output for a sine-wave input.

### Maximum peak output voltage range
The output of an op-amp can only operate within a certain voltage range without saturating to one of the supply rails or becoming non-linear. The range is specified as a positive and negative voltage limit and is dependent upon the load resistance connected to the output of the op-amp.

### Differential voltage gain
Is the ratio of the output voltage to the differential input voltage when no feedback is connected around the op-amp. It is typically in the region of 200,000.

### Load
Is the resistance connected between the output and 0V which is used when specifying the output voltage range.

# Uses of an op-amp
## *Inverting amplifier*

The voltage gain is equal to:

$$\text{GAIN} = \frac{\text{Vout}}{\text{Vin}} = -\frac{\text{R2}}{\text{R1}}$$

R3 should be = R1.R2 /(R1 + R2) so as to minimize effects of input offset current.

## *Non-inverting amplifier*

The voltage gain is equal to:

$$\text{GAIN} = \frac{\text{Vout}}{\text{Vin}} = 1 + \frac{\text{R2}}{\text{R1}}$$

R3 should be = R1.R2 /(R1 + R2) so as to minimize effects of input offset current.

## *Voltage follower*

The output voltage equals the input voltage without inversion. The main purpose of the voltage follower is to introduce current gain to buffer a load such as a meter from another circuit which may have a high enough voltage output signal but not enough current drive capability. The voltage follower has a very high input impedance and very low output impedance.

## *Summing amplifier*

The circuit opposite adds all three input voltages V1, V2, and V3 according to the equation:

$$\text{Vout} = -\text{R4} \left( \frac{\text{V1}}{\text{R1}} + \frac{\text{V2}}{\text{R2}} + \frac{\text{V3}}{\text{R3}} \right)$$

In order to minimize errors due to input offset current effects: 1/R5 = 1/R1 + 1/R2 + 1/R3.
The circuit may be used as an audio signal mixer.

## *Differential amplifier*

The differential amplifier (or subtractor) gives an output voltage which is proportional to the difference between the two inputs V1 and V2. In the example opposite, R2 = R4 and R1 = R3 and:

$$\text{Vout} = \frac{R2}{R1}\left(\ V2 - V1\ \right)$$

## *Differentiator*

$$\text{Vout} = -\ R1\ C1\ \frac{d\text{Vin}}{dt}$$

The differentiator (not to be confused with the differential amplifier) gives an output voltage which is proportional to the rate of change of the input voltage Vin. In practice, the above circuit suffers from the effects of high frequency noise and instability. In order to combat these effects a small resistor Rs is placed in series with C1. The integrator is then only applicable to frequencies much less than $1/(2\pi C1Rs)$.

## *Integrator*

$$Vout = -\frac{1}{R1 \; C1} \int Vin \; dt$$

The output voltage is the negative integral of the input voltage; if the input voltage is a steady dc negative value, the output will ramp positive in a linear manner. If the input is a steady positive dc value, the output will ramp negative in a linear manner.

In practice the above circuit suffers from the effects of small input offset voltages which are eventually integrated up and cause the output of the op amp to saturate to one of the supply rails. This problem is overcome by connecting a large value resistor (Rp) in parallel with C1 to define the gain at dc.

### *Voltage to constant current converter*

The circuit opposite is novel in that the output is not taken from the output of the op-amp but the non-inverting input (pin 3) The output is a constant current source which is proportional to the input voltage according to the equation:

$$Iout = \frac{Vin}{R3}$$

R1 = R2 = R3 = R4 and the supply rails are + and - 15V. The output load connected between pin 3 and 0V may be any resistance between a short circuit and 5k. Vin may be between - 10V and +10V. The circuit above gives a constant output current of +1mA when Vin = +10V.

### *Astable multivibrator (square wave oscillator)*

The circuit opposite produces an equal mark-space ratio square wave output with a peak to peak amplitude of approximately 25V when the supply rails are + and - 15V. The period of oscillation is given as:

$$2 \; C1 \; R1 \; Log_e \left( 1 + 2\frac{R3}{R2} \right)$$

## *Gyrator*

The gyrator synthesizes an inductor by the use of negative feedback via a capacitor. The input impedance looking into the two input terminals is:

$$2R + j\omega CR^2$$

i.e. a resistance of $2R$ in series with an inductance equal to $CR^2$.

## *Sine-wave oscillator*

R1, R2, C1 and C2 form a Wien network which sets the frequency of oscillation at:

$$f_{out} = \frac{1}{2\pi C1R1}$$

where R1 = R2 and C1 = C2

At the oscillation frequency, the voltage fed back to pin 3 of the op-amp is in phase with the output and attenuated to 1/3.

## *Precision half-wave rectifier*

A diode is unable to rectify signals adequately below its forward voltage drop of about 0.6V and ac signals of an amplitude of a few volts are distorted accordingly. The circuit above is able to half-wave rectify signals down to a fraction of a volt without distortion but gives 180 degree inversion. When the input signal is negative, pin 6 of the op-amp goes positive and causes D2 to conduct via R2 and R1. Vout is the same amplitude as Vin only inverted. The op-amp is always more positive than Vout by the forward voltage drop of D2. The non-linearity of D2 is compensated for by the op-amp as D2 is inside the feedback loop. When the input signal Vin goes positive, the output of the op-amp goes negative and D1 conducts. This causes D2 to be reverse biased and thus Vout = 0V (the same voltage as pin 2 of the op amp i.e. virtual earth). R4 gives a path for leakage current of D2.

## Design pitfalls when using op-amps

- Failure to de-couple the power supply rails as close as possible to the op-amp. This may cause the op-amp to oscillate or malfunction.

- Failure to balance the impedance levels at the two inputs. This may cause an offset voltage due to the input bias currents.

- 0V rail problems; the two inputs are connected to 0V points which have a voltage drop between them. In the circuit on the left, the power supply is connected so that the load current through R4 has to flow along the wire to which the inputs are connected. The load current produces a voltage drop $\Delta V$ across the small resistance of the wire and this appears in series with the signal V1. The op amp amplifies $\Delta V$ as well as the signal and the op amp may saturate, oscillate or latch up. The problem is solved by the circuit layout on the right where the power supply is connected so that the load current through R4 returns to the supply without flowing through the wire connected to the inputs of the op-amp.

## ✄ Testing an op-amp

An op-amp may not be tested using an analogue meter as per a transistor; the acid test is to connect the op-amp in a circuit it is suitable for.

## Single op-amps

All parameters are at 25°C and are worst case unless detailed otherwise

| TYPE No | SUPPLY | | INPUT VOLTAGE | | | | | INPUT CURRENT | | | | SLEW RATE | OUTPUT VOLTAGE | | |
|---------|--------|----|-----|------------|----------|----------|------|------|------|-----------|--------|-----------|-------|--------|------|
| | $V_{RAIL}$ | $I_q$ | $V_{OS}$ | $V_{OS}$ DRIFT typ | CM RANGE | DM RANGE | CMRR | BIAS | $I_{os}$ | $I_{os}$ DRIFT | RES | | RANGE | GAIN | LOAD |
| OP07C | ±15V | 5mA | 0.15mV | 1.8uV/°C | ±13Vmax | ±30Vmax | 100dB | ±7nA | 6nA | 50pA/°C | 8MΩ | 0.1V/uS | ±11.5V | 100V/mV | 2kΩ |
| OP27C | ±15V | 5.6mA | 0.1mV | 1.8uV/°C | ±11Vmax | - | 100dB | ±80nA | 75nA | 10pA/°C | 2GΩ | 1.7V/uS | ±11.5V | 700V/mV | 2kΩ |
| OP37C | ±15V | 5.6mA | 0.1mV | 1.8uV/°C | ±11Vmax | - | 100dB | ±80nA | 75nA | 10pA/°C | 2GΩ | 11V/uS | ±11.5V | 700V/mV | 2kΩ |
| TL061C | ±15V | .25mA | 15mV | 10uV/°C | ±11Vmax | ±30Vmax | 70dB | 400pA | 200pA | - | 1TΩ | 1.5V/uS | ±10V | 3V/mV | 10kΩ |
| TL071C | ±15V | 2.5mA | 10mV | 10uV/°C | ±11Vmax | ±30Vmax | 70dB | 200pA | 100pA | - | 1TΩ | 8V/uS | ±10V | 25V/mV | 2kΩ |
| TL081C | ±15V | 2.8mA | 15mV | 10uV/°C | ±11Vmax | ±30Vmax | 70dB | 400pA | 200pA | - | 1TΩ | 8V/uS | ±10V | 15V/mV | 2kΩ |
| LM301A | ±15V | 3mA | 7.5mV | 30uV/°C | ±12Vmax | ±30Vmax | 70dB | 250nA | 50nA | 1nA/°C | 0.5MΩ | 0.4V/uS | ±10V | 25V/mV | 2kΩ |
| LM308A | ±15V | 0.8mA | 7.5mV | 30uV/°C | ±14Vmax | - | 80dB | 7nA | 1nA | 10pA/°C | 10MΩ | 0.3V/uS | ±13V | 25V/mV | 10kΩ |
| AD548C | ±15V | 0.2mA | 0.25mV | 2uV/°C | ±11Vmax | ±20Vmax | 76dB | 10pA | 5pA | - | 1TΩ | 1.8V/uS | ±11V | 150V/mV | 5kΩ |
| uA709M | ±15V | 5.5mA | 5mV | 3uV/°C | ±8Vmax | ±5Vmax | 70dB | 500nA | 200nA | - | 0.15MΩ | - | ±10V | 25V/mV | 2kΩ |
| uA741C | ±15V | 2.8mA | 6mV | 10uV/°C | ±12Vmax | ±30Vmax | 70dB | 500nA | 200nA | 0.2nA/°C | 0.3MΩ | 0.5V/uS | ±10V | 20V/mV | 2kΩ |
| CA3130E | ±8V | 2mA | 8mV | - | - | ±8V | 90dB | 5pA | 0.5pA | - | 1.5TΩ | 10V/uS | ±10V | 300V/mV | 2kΩ |
| CA3140E | ±15V | 4mA | 5mV | - | - | ±8V | 90dB | 10pA | 0.5pA | - | 1.5TΩ | 9V/uS | ±10V | 100V/mV | 2kΩ |
| NE5534 | ±15V | 6.5mA | 2mV | 5uV/°C | ±12Vmax | ±0.5Vmax | 70dB | 500nA | 200nA | 0.2nA/°C | 50kΩ | 13V/uS typ | ±12V | 50V/mV | 600Ω |

# Voltage regulators

## 100mA positive voltage regulators

| PIN-OUT | TYPE No | INPUT VOLTAGE RANGE | OUTPUT VOLTAGE 1mA<Iout<70mA min<Vin<max | LINE REGULATION min<Vin<max | LOAD REGULATION 1mA<Iout<100mA | θJA | CIRCUIT |
|---|---|---|---|---|---|---|---|
| TO92 pin view | 78L05AC | 7V to 20V | 4.75Vmin, 5.25Vmax | 75mV max | 60mV max | 180 °C/W | |
| | 78L08AC | 10.5V to 23V | 7.6Vmin, 8.4Vmax | 100mV max | 80mV max | | |
| | 78L12AC | 14.5V to 27V | 11.4Vmin, 12.6V max | 180mV max | 100mV max | | |
| | 78L15AC | 17.5V to 30V | 14.25Vmin,15.75Vmax | 250mV max | 150mV max | | |
| | 78L18AC | 20.7V to 33V | 17.1Vmin, 18.9Vmax | 275mV max | 170mV max | | |
| | 78L24AC | 27V to 38V | 22.8Vmin, 25.2Vmax | 300mV max | 200mV max | | |

PIN-OUT: TO92 pin view — input, output, common

CIRCUIT: Input — 330nF — 78LxxAC — 100nF — Output, Common

## 100mA negative voltage regulators

| PIN-OUT | TYPE No | INPUT VOLTAGE RANGE | OUTPUT VOLTAGE 1mA<Iout<70mA min<Vin<max | LINE REGULATION min<Vin<max | LOAD REGULATION 1mA<Iout<100mA | θJA | CIRCUIT |
|---|---|---|---|---|---|---|---|
| TO92 pin view | 79L05AC | -7V to -20V | -4.75Vmin, -5.25Vmax | 60mV max | 50mV max | 180 °C/W | |
| | 79L12AC | -14.5V to -27V | -11.4Vmin, -12.6V max | 45mV max | 100mV max | | |
| | 79L15AC | -17.5V to -30V | -14.25Vmin,-15.75Vmax | 45mV max | 125mV max | | |
| | 79L18AC | -20.7V to -33V | -17.1Vmin, -18.9Vmax | 50mV max | 150mV max | | |
| | 79L24AC | -27V to -38V | -22.8Vmin, -25.2Vmax | 60mV max | 200mV max | | |

PIN-OUT: TO92 pin view — output, common, input

CIRCUIT: Input — 330nF — 79LxxAC — 100nF — Output, Common

Source - National Semiconductor

**1A positive voltage regulators**

| PIN-OUT TOP VIEW | TYPE No | INPUT VOLTAGE RANGE | OUTPUT VOLTAGE 5mA<Iout<1A min<Vin<max | LINE REGULATION min<Vin<max | LOAD REGULATION 5mA<Iout<1.5A | θJA | θJC | CIRCUIT |
|---|---|---|---|---|---|---|---|---|
| TO220 tab is common | **7805** | 8V to 20V | 4.65Vmin, 5.35Vmax | 50mV max | 100mV max | 65 degC/W | 5 degC/W | |
| | **7808** | 11.5V to 23V | 7.6Vmin, 8.4Vmax | 80mV max | 100mV max | | | |
| | **7812** | 15.5V to 27V | 11.4Vmin, 12.6V max | 120mV max | 120mV max | | | |
| | **7815** | 18.5V to 30V | 14.25Vmin, 15.75Vmax | 150mV max | 150mV max | | | |
| | **7818** | 22V to 33V | 17.1Vmin, 18.9Vmax | 180mV max | 180mV max | | | |
| | **7824** | 28V to 38V | 22.8Vmin, 25.2Vmax | 240mV max | 240mV max | | | |

**1A negative voltage regulators**

| PIN-OUT TOP VIEW | TYPE No | INPUT VOLTAGE RANGE | OUTPUT VOLTAGE 5mA<Iout<1A min<Vin<max | LINE REGULATION min<Vin<max | LOAD REGULATION 5mA<Iout<1.5A | θJA | θJC | CIRCUIT |
|---|---|---|---|---|---|---|---|---|
| TO220 tab is input | **7905C** | -7V to -20V | -4.75Vmin, -5.25Vmax | 100mV max | 100mV max | 65 degC/W | 5 degC/W | |
| | **7908C** | -10.5V to -23V | -7.6Vmin, -8.4Vmax | 160mV max | 160mV max | | | |
| | **7912C** | -14.5V to -27V | -11.4Vmin, -12.6V max | 240mV max | 240mV max | | | |
| | **7915C** | -17.5V to -30V | -14.25Vmin, -15.75Vmax | 300mV max | 300mV max | | | |
| | **7918C** | -21V to -33V | -17.1Vmin, -18.9Vmax | 360mV max | 360mV max | | | |
| | **7924C** | -27V to -38V | -22.8Vmin, -25.2Vmax | 480mV max | 480mV max | | | |

# 555 timer

## Equivalent circuit

## NE555

| | |
|---|---|
| **Power supply:** | 4.5V to 16V  (always fit a de-coupling capacitor directly across IC) |
| **Supply current:** | 15mA max at Vcc = 15V,  6mA max at Vcc = 5V |
| **Output drive current:** | ± 200 mA |

*Monostable mode*                    *Astable mode*

# Logic circuits

Logic circuits are digital computational circuits based on the functions: AND, OR, NAND, NOR, and memory and counting devices which may be connected to form a digital control or computational system such as a industrial production line controller or a computer. One two logic states are used, 1 or 0. Logic circuits were first implemented using thermionic valves and then later, using discrete transistor circuits. The first integrated circuit "family" of logic circuits was transistor-transistor logic or TTL which was based on multi-emitter bipolar integrated transistors. The table below summarizes the electrical parameters of the logic families currently available today.

| FAMILY | TTL | | | | CMOS | | | ECL | |
|---|---|---|---|---|---|---|---|---|---|
| | **74** | **74LS** | **74AS** | **74ALS** | **4000B** | **74HC** | **74HCT** | **10k** | **100k** |
| **SUPPLY** | 5.0V | 5.0V | 5.0V | 5.0V | 3-15V | 5.0V | 5.0V | -5.2V | -4.2V |
| $V_{IH}$ (min) | 2.0V | 2.0V | 2.0V | 2.0V | $0.7V_{cc}$ | 3.5V | 2.0V | -1.2V | -1.2V |
| $V_{IL}$ (max) | 0.8V | 0.8V | 0.8V | 0.8V | $0.3V_{cc}$ | 5.0V | 5.0V | -5.2V | -4.2V |
| $V_{OH}$ (min) | 2.4V | 2.7V | 2.7V | 2.7V | $V_{cc}$-0.05 | 4.9V | 4.9V | -0.9V | -0.9V |
| $V_{OL}$ (max) | 0.4V | 0.5V | 0.5V | 0.5V | 0.05V | 0.1V | 0.1V | -1.7V | -1.7V |
| $I_{IH}$ (max) | 0.04mA | 0.02mA | 0.2mA | 0.02mA | 0.3uA | 0.1uA | 0.1uA | | |
| $I_{IL}$ (max) | 1.6mA | 0.4mA | 2mA | 0.1mA | 0.3uA | 0.1uA | 0.1uA | | |
| $I_{OH}$ (max) | 0.4mA | 0.4mA | 2mA | 0.4mA | 3mA | 4mA | 4mA | 50mA | 55mA |
| $I_{OL}$ (max) | 16mA | 8mA | 20mA | 8mA | 3mA | 4mA | 4mA | 50mA | 55mA |
| mW/GATE | 10mW | 2mW | 8mW | 1mW | ≅0 | ≅0 | ≅0 | 25mW | 40mW |
| DELAY | 10nS | 10nS | 1.5nS | 4nS | 60nS | 30nS | 10nS | 2nS | 0.75nS |
| FAN-OUT | 10 | 20 | 10 | 20 | >100 | >100 | >100 | 10 | 10 |

All parameters are at 25 degrees C and nominal power supply voltage (15V for CMOS 4000B).

### Manufacturer's prefix letters

| | |
|---|---|
| CD | HARRIS |
| DM | NATIONAL SEMICONDUCTOR |
| HD | HITACHI |
| HEF | PHILIPS COMPONENTS |
| M74 | SGS THOMSON |
| MC | MOTOROLA |
| MM | NATIONAL SEMICONDUCTOR |
| N74F | PHILIPS COMPONENTS |
| PC74 | PHILIPS COMPONENTS |
| SN | TEXAS INSTRUMENTS |
| T | SGS-THOMSON |
| TC | TOSHIBA |

## Logic symbols and definitions

| FUNCTION | SYMBOL | TRUTH TABLE A B C | | | BOOLEAN | DESCRIPTION |
|---|---|---|---|---|---|---|
| AND | | 0 0 0<br>1 0 0<br>0 1 0<br>1 1 1 | | | $A \cdot B = C$ | The output is logic 1 when both inputs are logic 1 otherwise the output is logic 0 |
| OR | | 0 0 0<br>1 0 1<br>0 1 1<br>1 1 1 | | | $A + B = C$ | The output is only logic 0 when both inputs are logic 0 otherwise the output is logic 1 |
| NAND | | 0 0 1<br>1 0 1<br>0 1 1<br>1 1 0 | | | $\overline{A \cdot B} = C$ | By De Morgan's theorem the NAND gate may be thought as an OR gate for 0's at the inputs |
| NOR | | 0 0 1<br>1 0 0<br>0 1 0<br>1 1 0 | | | $\overline{A + B} = C$ | By De Morgan's theorem the NOR gate may be thought as an AND gate for 0's at the inputs |
| BUFFER | | 0     0<br>1     1 | | | $A = C$ | The output is the same logic state as the input but may have higher current drive |
| INVERT | | 0     1<br>1     0 | | | $\overline{A} = C$ | The output is the inverse logic state of the input |
| EXCLUSIVE OR | | 0 0 0<br>1 0 1<br>0 1 1<br>1 1 0 | | | $\overline{A}.B + A.\overline{B}$ $= C$ | The output is a logic 1 when the two inputs are at different logic states |

| | | | | | |
|---|---|---|---|---|---|
| NAND R - S LATCH | | S R   Q $\overline{Q}$<br>0 0   1 1<br>1 0   0 1<br>0 1   1 0<br>1 1   No change | | The two inputs are normally held at logic 1 and the latch is set or reset by logic 0 pulses |
| NOR R - S LATCH | | S R   Q $\overline{Q}$<br>1 1   0 0<br>0 1   0 1<br>1 0   1 0<br>0 0   No change | | The two inputs are normally held at logic 0 and the latch is set or reset by logic 1 pulses |

**Decimal to binary to hexadecimal**

Hexadecimal is a number system based on the number 16 and is used as a shorthand method of recording large binary numbers; i.e.the binary number 1011 1111 1010 1000 may be represented by the hex BFA8.

| DECIMAL | BINARY | | | | HEX |
|---------|--------|--------|--------|--------|-----|
| | $2^3 = 8_{DECIMAL}$ | $2^2 = 4_{DECIMAL}$ | $2^1 = 2_{DECIMAL}$ | $2^0 = 1_{DECIMAL}$ | |
| 0 | 0 | 0 | 0 | 0 | 0 |
| 1 | 0 | 0 | 0 | 1 | 1 |
| 2 | 0 | 0 | 1 | 0 | 2 |
| 3 | 0 | 0 | 1 | 1 | 3 |
| 4 | 0 | 1 | 0 | 0 | 4 |
| 5 | 0 | 1 | 0 | 1 | 5 |
| 6 | 0 | 1 | 1 | 0 | 6 |
| 7 | 0 | 1 | 1 | 1 | 7 |
| 8 | 1 | 0 | 0 | 0 | 8 |
| 9 | 1 | 0 | 0 | 1 | 9 |
| 10 | 1 | 0 | 1 | 0 | A |
| 11 | 1 | 0 | 1 | 1 | B |
| 12 | 1 | 1 | 0 | 0 | C |
| 13 | 1 | 1 | 0 | 1 | D |
| 14 | 1 | 1 | 1 | 0 | E |
| 15 | 1 | 1 | 1 | 1 | F |

## Serial data transmission

Note that logic '0' is +12V.

The above timing diagram shows the serial transmission of 1100 1010.

| BAUD RATE | PERIOD OF EACH BIT |
|---|---|
| 110 | 9.091mS |
| 150 | 6.67mS |
| 300 | 3.33mS |
| 600 | 1.67mS |
| 1200 | 833uS |
| 2400 | 417uS |
| 4800 | 208uS |
| 9600 | 104uS |
| 19,200 | 52.08uS |

## ASCII code

| | | FIRST DIGIT | | | | | | | |
|---|---|---|---|---|---|---|---|---|---|
| | | 000 | 001 | 010 | 011 | 100 | 101 | 110 | 111 |
| SECOND DIGIT | HEX | 0 | 1 | 2 | 3 | 4 | 5 | 6 | 7 |
| 0000 | 0 | NUL | DLE | SP | 0 | @ | P | \ | p |
| 0001 | 1 | SOH | DC1 | ! | 1 | A | Q | a | q |
| 0010 | 2 | STX | DC2 | " | 2 | B | R | b | r |
| 0011 | 3 | ETX | DC3 | # | 3 | C | S | c | s |
| 0100 | 4 | EOT | DC4 | $ | 4 | D | T | d | t |
| 0101 | 5 | ENQ | NAK | % | 5 | E | U | e | u |
| 0110 | 6 | ACK | SYN | & | 6 | F | V | f | v |
| 0111 | 7 | BEL | ETB | ' | 7 | G | W | g | w |
| 1000 | 8 | BS | CAN | ( | 8 | H | X | h | x |
| 1001 | 9 | HT | EM | ) | 9 | I | Y | i | y |
| 1010 | A | LF | SUB | * | : | J | Z | j | z |
| 1011 | B | VT | ESC | + | ; | K | [ | k | { |
| 1100 | C | FF | FS | , | < | L | \ | l | l |
| 1101 | D | CR | GS | - | = | M | ] | m | } |
| 1110 | E | SO | RS | . | > | N | ^ | n | ~ |
| 1111 | F | SI | US | / | ? | O | _ | o | DEL |

***Example:*** The ASCII code for capital letter "K" would be $4B_{hex}$ or 0100 1011 binary. The first binary bit may be used as a parity check however.

# 5 Circuit concepts

## Voltage source

An ideal voltage source (ac or dc) has zero internal resistance Rs so that the output voltage remains constant irrespective of the current drawn from the output.

*Example:* 3 terminal voltage regulator such as the 7805 is an excellent dc voltage source whose output remains virtually constant for output currents up to about 1 amp whereupon the device current limits and the output voltage falls.

## Current source

An ideal current source has infinite source resistance so that the output current is constant irrespective of the load resistance applied to the output. A 1A current source may be thought of as a voltage source of say 10,000,000 volts with a source resistance of 10 Megohms. Load resistances of 0 to say 100 ohms will not cause the output current to change significantly.

*Example:* The drain circuit of a field-effect transistor is a good current source as the drain current is hardly affected by changes in resistance in the drain circuit.

## Potential divider

Is formed by two series connected impedances (not necessarily resistors). In the circuit opposite, the voltage Vout is equal to $V1 \times R2/(R1 + R2) = 10V \times 10k / 20k = 5V$.

A standard x10 oscilloscope probe uses the potential divider concept. An oscilloscope input impedance is usually standardized at 1M in parallel with 1000pF (R2 and C2 in the figure opposite). A 9M resistor in the scope probe would make a potential divider with the 1 M input impedance of the scope and would give the required 1/10 potential division. At high frequencies however, there would be a greater attenuation of the signal V1 due to the input capacitance of the scope C2. To overcome this, a capacitor C1 is fitted in the scope probe which acts as a capacitance potential divider with C2. The probe capacitor C1, is made to be adjustable so it can be made to give an exact attenuation of 1/10 with C2 at high frequencies.

## Voltage gain and current gain

The voltage gain aspect of an amplifier is exhibited from input to output; i.e. a signal voltage is applied to the input and a greater amplitude version of the signal appears at the output.

The current gain aspect of a power amplifier is usually exhibited from output to input. The current gain will not be seen until a load is connected which draws current from the output. The input of the amplifier will then demand a current which is equal to the output current divided by the current gain.

## Diode pump

THE OUTPUT VOLTAGE IS SET BY $C_1$ AND THE FREQUENCY
THE OUTPUT RIPPLE IS SET BY $C_2$

The diode pump gives a dc output which is dependent upon the peak to peak ac input voltage and its frequency. Any dc component on the input waveform is ignored. It may be used as a crude frequency to voltage converter or to create a low voltage dc power supply from a higher voltage ac supply such as the 240V mains supply.

On each cycle of the input signal, charge is collected on C1 and then dumped into C2. The charge on C2 is constantly leaking away through R1. Equilibrium is reached when the charge gained by C2 from C1 equals the charge lost by C2 into R1. If C2 is made large so that there is a small ripple present at Vout, then Vout may be considered constant. The charge gained by C2 is the charge lost by C1 on each cycle of the input waveform. When the input waveform is at -30V, then C1 is charged to 30V. When the positive edge of the input waveform occurs, the right hand plate of C1 would be raised by 30V if D2 was not in circuit. D2 does conduct however and charge flows from C1 to C2. D2 turns off when the right hand plate of C1 is discharged to a voltage equal to Vout.

| Charge lost by $C_1$ | $= C_1$ x change in V across $C_1$ |
| --- | --- |
| | $= C_1 ( 30 - V_{out})$ |

Charge lost by $C_2$ during one period T of the input square wave is
$$= I T \quad \text{(where I is the current drawn by } R_1 \text{ and is } = \text{Vout} / R_1).$$

| Charge lost = charge gained |
| --- |
| $V_{out}T / R1 = C1 ( 30 - V_{out} )$ |
| $V_{out} = \dfrac{30}{1 + 1 / (fR1C1)}$ |

Where $f = 1/T$.

## Negative feedback

May be used to improve the performance of amplifiers. A fraction of the output signal of an amplifier is subtracted from the input signal before it is applied to the input of the amplifier. The resulting improvements are:

- A reduction in the variations in gain of the amplifier due to temperature, age, and variations in components in the amplifier.
- Increase in bandwidth.
- Reduction in distortion.
- The output and input impedances are altered.

### *Example 1: single NPN transistor amplifier*

The input voltage is applied between the base and the emitter of the transistor. The input impedance of the transistor is very low and depends upon the input voltage. Input voltages of no more than a fraction of a volt may be applied. The output of the transistor is its collector current Ic. This also flows out of the emitter. In order to produce an output voltage of the amplifier a resistor R1 is used to convert the output current to a voltage. The resulting voltage amplifier is very non-linear and drifts severely with variations in temperature. If a different transistor is used, the amplifier's performance will be changed dramatically.

### *With negative feedback (the emitter follower)*

The input voltage to the total stage is now applied between the base of TR1 and 0V. Consequently the input to the transistor (between its base and emitter) is equal to the input voltage to the stage minus the output voltage. The entire output voltage has been fed back in series with the input of the transistor and it is of the opposite polarity to the input to the stage. In this circuit 100% negative feedback has been employed. The result is a stage which has a voltage gain of 1 but is very linear and insensitive to temperature changes and different transistors. More importantly, the input impedance has been increased and the output impedance has been reduced.

### *Example 2: operational amplifier*

IC1 is connected as an inverting amplifier. It has a voltage gain of approximately 200,000 but a bandwidth of only 10Hz. The voltage gain drifts wildly with temperature and if a different op amp is used, the gain may change by up to 10 times. The amplifier is said to be operating on open-loop and is never used in a linear application in this manner.

### *With negative feedback*

R3 provides negative shunt feedback which reduces the voltage gain to 10 however the bandwidth has been increased to 100kHz and the gain is almost independent of the operational amplifier's gain and is now largely dependent upon the resistors R1 and R3. The output impedance has been reduced, but the input impedance is now R1 due to the virtual earth effect.

## Positive feedback

Is sometimes referred to as regenerative feedback. A fraction of the output signal of an amplifier is added to the input signal and in phase with the input signal before it is applied to the input of the amplifier. Positive feedback is less common today compared to when amplifying devices were more expensive. Positive feedback was used to increase the gain of an amplifying stage or stages, however it has the drawback that the total circuit could become unstable and self-oscillate.

Positive feedback is more commonly used in comparator circuits where it is employed to eliminate the effects of noise on an analogue signal which is being compared with a threshold level.

In the circuit above, the input voltage is a slowly varying dc signal which may represent the temperature of a room. IC1 is connected as a comparator which compares the dc input signal with a 5V reference. When the input voltage exceeds 5V, then the output of IC1 switches from negative to positive saturation. If the input signal contains noise, then the input signal may vary above and below the 5V reference when it is in the region of 5V. This will cause the output of IC1 to rapidly switch between positive and negative saturation which may not be desirable if the op-amp is controlling a high power device via a relay. The relay would be made to switch in and out very quickly which could lead to premature contact wear.

In the modified circuit above, positive feedback has been added via R3. The input to the op-amp is now the addition of the input signal and approximately 10% of the output signal. When the input signal reaches 5V, the output of the op-amp switches to positive saturation and adds to the input signal. The input to pin 3 is consequently elevated by the positive feedback and quickly raised above the 5V threshold level. The effects of any noise on the input signal are therefore reduced. A similar phenomenon occurs when the input signal is falling. The net result is that the circuit switches on a higher input signal when it is increasing to that when it is decreasing. The effect is often referred to as hysteresis.

**Miller effect**

In figure (a) below, the lower plate of C1 may be considered to be stationary and the upper plate is being varied in voltage by V1. As V1 varies, a current flows to charge and discharge the capacitor according to the equation **i = C1 dv/dt.** The voltage generator "sees" a capacitance of C1. When a second voltage generator V2, equal in magnitude, frequency and phase to V1, is inserted as shown in figure (b), both plates of the capacitor are varying in sympathy. No current will flow from V1 and voltage generator V1 "sees" zero capacitance. If V2 is reversed as in figure (c), then the magnitude of the voltage across C1 is twice what it was in figure (a). The voltage generator V1 actually "sees" 2 x C1.

(a)     (b)     (c)

All semiconductor junctions have capacitance. This cannot be entirely avoided during manufacture. The base-emitter junction of a bipolar transistor for example will have capacitance and when the transistor is used in the common emitter mode, the base-emitter capacitance will cause current to be bypassed to 0V at higher frequencies when its reactance is in the same order as the base resistor. This will reduce the gain of the stage.

The transistor's collector-base junction also has capacitance and if the voltage at the collector was not varying then the capacitance "seen" at the input would simply be the collector-base capacitance because the plate of the capacitor which is connected to the collector may be considered to be at 0V (ac wise). The voltage at the collector is varying however as this is the output voltage of the circuit. The capacitance "seen" at the input is actually magnified by an amount equal to (1 + the voltage gain of the circuit) This is the Miller effect.

## Bootstrapping

Could be considered to be the opposite of the Miller effect. In the previous section it was seen that the Miller effect increased the effective value of the collector-base capacitance because the collector was moving in antiphase to the input signal. The effective value would have been reduced if the collector had been moving in phase with the input signal. The concept would be the same if the parameter in question were resistance rather than capacitance.

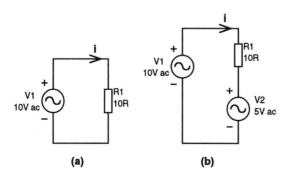

(a)          (b)

In diagram (a) above, the ac voltage source V1 "sees" R1 as being 10 ohms. In diagram (b) the ac voltage source V2 is exactly the same frequency and phase as V1. The current i is therefore 10V - 5V divided by 10R = 0.5A. V1 "sees" 20 ohms. The voltage source V1 is unaware that the other end of R1 is connected to V2 and so V1 "sees" 20 ohms (10V / 0.5A = 20R) The other end of R1 is being bootstrapped by V2. Bootstrapping increases the effective value of a resistor (or in fact any impedance). The technique may also be used to reduce stray capacitances in a circuit.

The concept of bootstrapping was given its name by the bizarre idea that a person could defy gravity by pulling himself up by his own bootstraps thereby reducing his own weight by however hard he pulled.

# 6  Electromagnetic compatibility

*Definition*

Electromagnetic compatibility (EMC) is the subject which considers how an item of electrical or electronic equipment may:

1.  Interfere with other electrical or electronic equipment due to it generating electromagnetic interference.

> This is called
> **The emission aspect**

2.  Be interfered with by other electrical or electronic equipment or phenomenon which generates electromagnetic interference.

> This is called
> **The immunity aspect**

Depending upon the type of equipment, standards are being prepared or have been published which detail the maximum levels of interference for both aspects of EMC.

Electromagnetic interference generated by equipment may be transmitted to other equipment:

1.  Via interconnecting cable e.g. the mains supply.

> This is called
> **Conducted interference**

2.  Through space by electromagnetic waves.

> This is called
> **Radiated interference**

Up to a frequency of approximately 30MHz, interference signals are usually propagated by conduction through interconnecting cables. (This is sometimes called galvanic coupling). Above 30MHz, interference signals are usually propagated by radiation.

## Design guidelines to reduce emission

In general it is rate of change of current which generates the severest interference. High switching speed semiconductors are the greatest source of conducted and radiated interference. If high switching speed is not required, the best design maxim is to reduce di/dt.
   If fast switching is unavoidable the following guidelines should be followed:

* Ensure that de-coupling capacitors are fitted close to the fast switching devices.

* Avoid "loops" in the printed circuit board which carry the fast current transients or "edges".

* Mount the circuit inside a screened metal box.

* Class Y capacitors may be necessary to provide a return path for interference currents flowing from the circuit to the metal box via stray capacitances.

- Fit a class X capacitor across the incoming mains supply to de-couple high frequency components of the input current demand.

- Add series inductors to further encourage high frequency components of current to flow from de-coupling capacitors rather than from the power supply.

*Example showing methods of reduction of emission.*

The above circuit is a half-bridge inverter which runs at approximately 30kHz and is used to transform mains power down to 12V to operate a tungsten-halogen lamp. The two transistors TR1 and TR2 generate interference due to the fact that they are switching current at high speed. In order to reduce emission, the following guidelines apply:

- C5, C6 and C7 are high frequency de-coupling; they should be a low inductance type and should be mounted close to TR1 and TR2.

- Avoid creating loops in the printed circuit board in the tracks that carry the current from C5, C6 and C7 to TR1 and TR2.

- Fit a class X de-coupling capacitor C3 to further prevent the high frequency harmonics of current (due to the fast "edges" of current) from being drawn from the mains.

- Insert chokes L1 and L2 to introduce a series impedance to fast "edges" of current. L1 and L2 further encourage the high frequency harmonics of current to flow through C3.

- If the circuit is mounted in a metal box, the box must be earthed for safety reasons. The box will then reduce the amount of radiated interference by screening. The circuit will have stray capacitance to the box however (C stray) which will cause interference currents to flow into the earth connection of the mains and may cause interference to other equipment. Class Y capacitors C1 and C2 should therefore be fitted so as to bypass the current and prevent it flowing into the mains earth.

### Design guidelines to improve immunity

- Use lower value resistors where a choice is available (for example when biasing the inputs of op-amps). This will increase the supply current of the circuit however.

- Use a differential input stage to reject common-mode interference.

- Fit de-coupling capacitors on susceptible inputs.

- Use screened cable to connect items of equipment.

- Fit ferrite beads over input cables which may be susceptible.

- Mount circuit in an earthed metal box.

- Avoid making two 0V connections between two items of equipment (e.g. mains earths are commoned and equipments are also connected via the screen of a connecting cable.

- Add further dc rail de-coupling capacitors at high gain stages.

# 7 Sound

Sound waves are longitudinal wave vibrations usually in air, i.e. air vibrates in the same direction to which the sound wave is travelling. The audible frequency range is approximately 20Hz to 20kHz depending upon the individual. The upper limit is related to age; a young person's hearing may extend to 20kHz however an old person may only be able to hear up to 6kHz or less.

The dynamic range of sound is measured in decibels where 1dB = 10 times the logarithm of the ratio of the power levels of the loudest sound to the quietest sound. The dynamic range of sound levels in a classical music performance may be from 30 dB during very quiet passages to 100 dB during the 1812 overture. (a range of 70dB).

The range of sound levels occurring in everyday life is shown in the table below.

| DECIBELS | PRESSURE | | EXAMPLES |
|----------|----------|------------------|--------------------------|
| 120 | 20Pa | THRESHOLD OF PAIN | JET AIRCRAFT AT 500 FT |
| 110 | | | POPULAR MUSIC BAND |
| 100 | 2Pa | | INSIDE A TUBE TRAIN |
| 90 | | | BUSY STREET |
| 80 | 0.2Pa | | WORKSHOP |
| 70 | | | NOISY OFFICE |
| 60 | 0.02Pa | | NORMAL CONVERSATION |
| 50 | | | QUIET OFFICE |
| 40 | 0.2uPa | | RURAL HOUSE |
| 30 | | | QUIET CONVERSATION |
| 20 | 2uPa | | WHISPER |
| 10 | | | STILL NIGHT IN THE COUNTRY |
| 0 | 20uPa | THRESH. OF HEARING | SOUND-PROOF ROOM |

The decibel is actually a ratio:

$$1dB = 10 \times Log\ P1/P2\ \text{(ratio of two power levels)}$$
$$1dB = 20 \times Log\ V1/V2\ \text{(ratio of two voltage levels)}$$

The above table is based on 0dB being a sound pressure of 20uPascals = 200udynes/cm$^2$
Other decibel systems in use are:

dBm: (based on 0dB = 1mW)
dBu: (based on 0dB = 0.775V rms)
dBV: (based on 0dB = 1V rms)
dBW: (based on 0dB = 1W)

**Glossary of audio terms**

*Compression*

The dynamic range of a signal is compressed i.e. quiet sounds are made louder, loud sounds are made quieter. The gain of a compressor is inversely dependent upon the input signal. It is used to enable signals which have large variations in sound level (e.g. a symphony orchestra) to be processed by a system which has a limited range of levels (e.g. an a.m. radio transmission system)

*Graphic equalizer*

Is a comprehensive tone control system where the audio frequency range is divided into specific bands and each band may be controlled by a potentiometer which enables the frequencies in the band to be boosted or attenuated. Each band is centred on one particular frequency which receives the greatest boost or cut with reducing effects to the frequencies either side of the centre frequency at a rate which depends upon the design of the equalizer.

*Harmonic distortion*

Is where additional frequency signals are introduced by an audio system which are multiples of the frequencies of the true signals being processed. The distortion is introduced because of non-linearities in the audio system.

*Limiter*

Is an electronic circuit which processes a signal so that levels below a pre-set threshold are unaltered, but signals exceeding the threshold are reduced in dynamic range to prevent them exceeding a certain maximum value. It is used to ensure that clipping does not occur in a subsequent amplification system.

*Pink noise*

Has equal noise power per octave of the audible frequency range. It is used to evaluate graphic equalizers as equal amplitudes of noise are applied to each band.

*Power amplifier*

Supplies the necessary voltage gain and current gain to enable a specified power to be supplied to the specified load (e.g. a loudspeaker). A typical audio power amplifier will give its rated power output into say a 4 ohm load with an input signal of 0.775 volts (0dBu).

*Pre-amplifier*

*Is used:*
- to match the input transducer to the later stages of the main amplifier,
- to correct any frequency characteristic that has been made to the signal,
- to modify the frequency characteristics to suit listening conditions,
- to provide sufficient voltage gain and current gain to drive the input of a power amplifier.

*Signal to noise ratio*

Is the ratio in decibels of the average signal level in volts (Vs) to the total noise voltage (Vn) S/N ratio = 20 Log Vs/Vn.

*White noise*

Is equal noise power per Hz over the complete audio frequency range.

# Pre-amplifier

The circuit shown above was designed for either a disco, vinyl-record, crystal pick-up or a guitar. Although the use of the 741 op-amp may be adequate for stage amplification, the use of a higher slew-rate and lower noise device may be preferred for the more critical performer. A suitable device would be a TL071 or TL081.

113

# Power amplifiers

There are many different configurations of power amplifiers, however there are six main stages or sections which are common to most power amplifier designs.

- Power modulators - output circuit (TR3 to TR6).
- Biasing circuit determining the class of operation (X).
- Biasing circuit determining the quiescent conditions (R1 & R2).
- AC gain determining circuit (R3, R4, C2).
- Bootstrap circuit or similar to improve power efficiency (C3).
- Coupling of the load (C4).

### Power modulators (TR3 to TR6)

These are the output devices and give most of the current gain and very little voltage gain. The configuration shown above is a complementary emitter follower. Other possible configurations are shown below.

COMPLEMENTARY COMMON EMITTER     QUASI-COMPLEMENTARY

Sometimes Darlington pairs are used to increase the current gain but more recently power MOSFET devices are used for the output devices as they provide a very high current gain and are voltage driven.

**Biasing circuit determining the class of operation (X)**

In all cases the class of operation depends upon the bias voltage between the two input bases. The transfer admittance (collector current out for base-emitter voltage in) characteristic of a transistor is very non-linear at very low voltage levels and an offset voltage is required between the two input bases of the power devices to overcome the non-linearity which is termed cross-over distortion. Two of the more common means of producing the required offset voltage are shown below.

VAB = 4Vd                Vbe MULTIPLIER VAB=Vbe(1+R1/R2)

These circuits are often in thermal contact with the output devices so that the offset voltage tracks changes in Vbe's with temperature.

**Biasing circuit determining the quiescent conditions (R1 and R2)**

In order to ensure that the amplifier clips the power supply rails equally for positive and negative voltage swings, the output quiescent dc voltage level should be set exactly half way between the power rails. The quiescent point is set by R1 and R2 and its stability is ensured by 100% dc negative feedback via R3. TR1 compares the output quiescent dc voltage with that set by R1 and R2 and adjusts the output accordingly via the intermediate stages. The function of TR1 is often accomplished by a differential amplifier such as a long-tailed pair or an op-amp.

**AC gain determining circuit (R3, R4, C2)**

Power amplifiers usually require voltage gains in the order of 10 to 50. The overall negative feedback for ac signals is set to the required percentage by the potential division of R3 and R4. C2 blocks dc and hence the overall feedback for dc is 100%.

**Bootstrap circuit or similar to improve power efficiency (C3)**

When the output swing of the amplifier is positive, TR3 is turned on by base current via R5 in series with R6. In order that the output voltage of the amplifier can swing as close to the positive rail as possible, the total value of R5 and R6 must be made very low. This may cause over-dissipation in the resistors and TR2. The bootstrap capacitor C3, "hoists" the junction of R5 and R6 above the positive supply rail each time the output attempts to swing positive. This provides the necessary positive base drive for TR3.

**Coupling the load (C4)**

The quiescent output of the amplifier is half the supply voltage. If a load was directly connected to the output, an unwanted dc current would flow. C4 blocks the dc whilst allowing ac power to the load. Alternative arrangements would be to use positive and negative dc power rails which would allow direct connection of the load between the output and 0V. Another arrangement would be to connect the load to the centre point of two capacitors in series which are connected across the dc supply rail.

# Electronics and music

Musical notes are made up from combinations of sine-wave vibrations. Some musical instruments such as the flute give almost pure sine-tones. In addition to the note being played, most instruments generate harmonics or overtones which are usually related to the fundamental note by exact multiples of its frequency. The human ear is able to analyse the different harmonic pattern of each instrument to tell them apart even though they may be playing the same note. Fourier analysis is ideally applicable to the sound of musical instruments.

Musical instruments also differ in the characteristics of attack and decay of the sound. Plucked instruments have a very fast attack; bowed instruments take longer to "sound"

- The audible frequency range is approximately 20Hz to 20kHz depending upon the individual.
- A doubling in frequency of a note is termed an octave in music.

- In western music, the octave is divided into 12 notes.

- On keyboard and fretted instruments, the interval between each note is the 12th root of 2. This is termed the scale of equal temperament as there is the same frequency ratio between one note and the next. This scale does not give the purest harmonies however. "Analogue" instruments such as a violin can play the true harmonies and sound more pleasing to the trained musical ear.

### Electronic effects in popular music

#### *Fuzz*
The waveform of the instrument, (usually an electric guitar) is deliberately clipped or square wave tones are generated which are equal in frequency to the note being played. The waveform may be clipped in the pre-amp stages of the amplifier by connecting back to back zener diodes across the feedback resistor of an op-amp stage. Fuzz was first popularized by the Rolling Stones in their recording of "(I can't get no) satisfaction".

#### *Wah-wah*
The instrument is played through a narrow bandpass filter whose centre frequency may be shifted up and down the frequency spectrum usually by a foot pedal device.

#### *Phasing or chorus effect*
The signal from the instrument is delayed and then mixed with the undelayed signal. Some frequencies are shifted in phase by 180 degrees and are cancelled out. A notch comb filter is created having notches an octave apart. If the delay is varies slowly and in a ramp fashion, the phasing effect is produced which is similar to the "jet-plate" effect heard when listening to a short-wave radio station which is fading and increasing in strength due to the ground wave and sky waves adding and cancelling. This effect was first popularized by the band The Small Faces in their recording "Itchycoo Park".

If the delay is varied in a more random manner, the chorus effect is produced where the impression of many instruments playing simultaneously is created. This may be explained by considering many violins playing the same note simultaneously; the waveforms will vary in phase and some harmonic frequencies will add and some will cancel at random.

### Tremelo

Tremelo is amplitude modulation of the instrument's sound and it is created electronically by varying the gain of the amplifier in a low frequency sinusoidal manner at about 2 to 5 Hz. Certain cultures in the world use tremelo in the voice when singing.

### Vibrato

Vibrato is frequency modulation and it is used by singers and musicians in western cultures. It is created by varying the pitch of the note up and down around the true pitch of the note being played or sung. It is created electronically in say an electronic organ, by varying the frequency of the oscillator which is generating the note being played.

### Reverberation

Occurs naturally in large halls when reflections from walls and ceilings of the sound of the performers arrive later in time than the direct sound. There is a multitude of reflections which all blend together to give a pleasing, sustaining effect to the sound. It may be created electronically by the use of acoustic spring delay lines or plates but more recently is created by delaying the sound using semiconductor devices.

### Echo

Is similar to reverberation but the sound reflections are fewer and are separately distinguishable. It may be created electronically by using magnetic tape-loop delay systems but more recently by using semiconductor devices.

**Mathematics of music**

| MUSICAL NOTE | TONIC SOL-FA | MUSICAL NAME | Scale of equal temperament | | Pure scale | | |
|---|---|---|---|---|---|---|---|
| | | | FREQUENCY Hz | FREQUENCY RATIO TO C | FREQUENCY Hz | FREQUENCY RATIO TO C | MUSICAL INTERVAL |
| C | Doh | TONIC | 261.63 | 1 | 261.63 | 1 | UNISON |
| C# | De | - | 277.19 | 1.059 | - | - | - |
| D | Ray | SUPER-TONIC | 293.67 | 1.122 | 294.33 | 9/8 = 1.125 | 2nd |
| D# | Re | - | 311.13 | 1.189 | 313.96 | 6/5 = 1.2 | Minor 3rd |
| E | Me | MEDIANT | 329.63 | 1.26 | 327.04 | 5/4 = 1.25 | 3rd |
| F | Fah | SUB-DOMINANT | 349.23 | 1.335 | 348.84 | 4/3 = 1.333 | 4th |
| F# | Fe | - | 370 | 1.414 | - | - | DIMINISHED 5th |
| G | Soh | DOMINANT | 392 | 1.498 | 392.45 | 3/2 = 1.5 | 5th |
| G# | Se | - | 415.31 | 1.587 | 418.61 | 8/5 = 1.6 | AUGMENTED 5th |
| A | Lah | SUB-MEDIANT | 440 | 1.682 | 436.05 | 5/3 = 1.666 | 6th |
| A# | Le | - | 466.17 | 1.782 | 470.93 | 9/5 = 1.8 | 7th |
| B | Te | LEADING NOTE | 493.89 | 1.888 | 490.56 | 15/8 = 1.875 | MAJOR 7th |
| C' | Doh' | TONIC | 523.26 | 2 | 523.26 | 2 | OCTAVE |

# Telephone

## Basic circuit of a telephone

- To ac, the telephone line is a 600 ohm balanced 2-wire transmission line.
- To dc, the telephone line is a 50V dc source with a source resistance of between 400 and 1660 ohms.
- An "on the hook" telephone is open circuit to dc.
- The bell or ringer is ac coupled to the line via a 1.8uF capacitor.
- The ringing voltage is approximately 75V r.m.s. 25Hz (or 16Hz).
- The telephone is "answered" by completing a dc circuit to the telephone line (usually via the mouthpiece).
- The side-tone transformer reduces the mouthpiece's signal level to the earpiece (so the speaker does not deafen himself) but does not attenuate incoming signals.
- "Old fashioned" dialling is called loop-disconnect; the dc path completed by lifting the hand-set is interrupted twice in quick succession for a digit "2", 3 times for a digit "3" and so on; (0 is 10 times).
- Tone dialling is accomplished by simultaneously transmitting two tones for each digit.

| DIGITS | | | | | LOW FREQUENCY |
|---|---|---|---|---|---|
| | 1 | 2 | 3 | A | 697Hz |
| | 4 | 5 | 6 | B | 770Hz |
| | 7 | 8 | 9 | C | 852Hz |
| | * | 0 | # | D | 941Hz |
| HIGH FREQUENCY | 1209Hz | 1336Hz | 1477Hz | 1633Hz | |

# 8 Light

**Visible light**

Visible light is in the wavelength range **380 - 760nm**.

**Luminous flux**

Is the rate of flow of luminous energy and is measured in lumens. One lumen of luminous flux at a wavelength of 400 nm corresponds to a radiated power of 3.5 watts. The light output of lamps is specified in lumens.

**Illumination**

When light hits a solid surface, the process is known as illumination. Illuminance is the luminous flux per unit area and is measured in lux. **1 lux = 1 lumen per square metre.**
In the USA the foot-candle is used where 1 foot-candle = 1 lumen /square foot = 10.76 lux.

| APPLICATION | SUGGESTED ILLUMINATION |
|---|---|
| EMERGENCY LIGHTING ESCAPE ROUTES | 0.2 LUX |
| STORAGE AREAS | 1-10 LUX |
| CAR PARKS, NON-CRITICAL WORK AREAS | 10-50 LUX |
| SPORTS PRACTICE, PLAYGROUNDS | 50-100 LUX |
| FACTORY ASSEMBLY AREAS | 300 LUX |
| GENERAL OFFICE WORK | 400-500 LUX |
| DRAWING OFFICES, INSPECTION AREAS | 750 LUX |
| SPORTING EVENTS FOR TV | 500-1000 LUX |

**Luminous intensity**

Is the measure of how much luminous flux is emitted within a small conical angle. Luminous intensity is measured in candelas. A spotlamp concentrates the light output into a narrow beam and so the luminous intensity when looking into the beam is high. A light bulb having the same lumen output would not give the same luminous intensity as the light is radiated over a much greater solid angle.

**Luminous efficacy**

Is a measure of the light output of a lamp per unit of electrical power consumed. It is measured in lumens per watt.

| LAMP TYPE | EFFICACY (LUMENS PER WATT) |
|---|---|
| GLS (LIGHT BULB) | 10 to 20 |
| TUNGSTEN HALOGEN | 12 to 22 |
| HIGH PRESSURE MERCURY (MBF) | 32 to 56 |
| FLUORESCENT | 68 to 80 |
| HIGH PRESSURE SODIUM (SON) | 55 to 120 |
| LOW PRESSURE SODIUM (SOX) | 70 to 125 |

# Electronics in lighting

An uninformed engineer may be of the opinion that the circuitry involved in lighting is no more complex than a light bulb and a switch. There are many applications of electronics to lighting however; to start and ballast certain light sources such as discharge lamps, to control when the illumination is required, and to control the lamp's intensity.

## Control of fluorescent lighting

A fluorescent lamp may not be connected directly to the 240V 50Hz mains supply. The current through the lamp must be limited. The most obvious way would be to use a resistor in series with the lamp, however the resistor would get very hot and the total efficacy (light output per watt of electricity) would be very poor. A capacitor could be used, but this solution would be subject to very large pulses of current through the lamp if the mains power was applied when it was at the peak of the sine-wave. An inductance in series with the lamp is used in practice and is referred to as a ballast. It is simply a coil of wire on a laminated iron core. If the circuit is connected to the mains supply, the lamp will not strike because the gas inside a fluorescent lamp ionizes (and so becomes conductive) at voltages much greater than the 240V mains supply. The lamp must be started and this is achieved by:

   1.   Heating the cathodes of the lamp to encourage them to emit electrons.
   2.   Applying a high voltage across the lamp to promote conduction through the gas.

The device used to perform this task is called a starter and it interacts with the ballast to achieve the starting process.

The starter is a bi-metallic strip contact set, encapsulated in a glass envelope which contains a gas. When power is first applied, the bi-metallic contacts are open circuit and a small current flows through the gas causing it to heat up. The bi-metallic contacts close causing a circuit to be connected via the cathodes of the lamp; the current is limited by the reactance of the ballast and the cathodes of the lamp are heated. The gas in the starter cools because the current is now flowing through the contacts. Eventually the contacts open and interrupt the current and because it is flowing in an inductive circuit, a high voltage is generated across the contacts and consequently across the lamp. If the lamp does not strike, then the process repeats until the lamp does conduct. When the lamp is conducting then the voltage across it is much lower than that needed to cause the gas in the starter to heat up, consequently the starter remains open circuit.

## Electronic starter

The glow starter is simple and cheap but has a limited life. It does not necessarily start the lamp first time and there may be several attempts accompanied by annoying flashing and flickering of the lamp before conduction is achieved. When the lamp fails, the glow starter makes repeated attempts to start the lamp which results in an incessant flicker. The electronic starter overcomes all of the drawbacks of the glow starter. The lighting industry seems to have standardized on the use of an electronic switch device called the Fluoractor which was pioneered by Texas Instruments. The Fluoractor is effectively a Darlington connected GTO pair of devices in parallel with a 1500V power zener. When power is first applied to the circuit, the Fluoractor device is triggered into conduction via R6, ZD1 and ZD2. Cathode heating of the lamp occurs via the Fluoractor in series with D5, D6 and D7. The voltage pedestal created by the forward voltage drop of D5, D6 and D7 causes C2 to be charged via R4 in series with R5. After a period of a second or so, the gate-source threshold voltage of the FET TR1 is reached, it turns on and causes the Fluoractor to be turned off by GTO action. When the Fluoractor turns off, the current it interrupts is flowing in an inductive circuit (the ballast) and consequently a high voltage back-emf is generated. This is clamped to 1500V by the power zener in the Fluoractor. The process repeats until the lamp strikes. The zener diode, ZD1, is selected to have a voltage which is greater than the running voltage of the lamp, consequently when the lamp is running, ZD1 will not conduct and the Fluoractor is prevented from further triggering.

**Electronic ballast**

The fluorescent lamp may be ballasted electronically at high frequency and has advantages over the wound ballast as follows:-

- Higher efficiency.
- Higher efficacy (more light output per watt input).
- Less flicker and a reported lower incidence of headaches of staff working in fluorescent light.
- Less weight than wound ballasts.
- No 50 Hz "buzz".

TR1, TR2 and T1 form a self oscillating inverter running at approximately 30kHz. It is "kick-started" by R1, C3 and the diac. D2 disables the kick-start when the inverter is running. The lamp is ballasted by L1 which is a small-size ferrite-cored inductor. C4 blocks dc to the lamp and C5 and the PTC give cathode heating. C5 resonates with L1 to provide a high voltage to start the lamp. During any one half cycle of the mains supply, C1 is charged via the diode bridge and discharged into the lamp at the frequency of the inverter. This improves the power factor of the circuit considerably. An input mains filter is desirable to reduce conducted r.f.i. into the mains supply. Integrated circuits are available to control the input mains current to further improve the power factor.

# High frequency inverter

Fluorescent lamps may be operated from a low voltage dc supply such as an automobile battery by means of a simple high frequency inverter circuit. The MOSFETs TR1 and TR2 form an astable multivibrator which operates at approximately 30kHz. The voltage is transformed up by T1 and C1 acts as the current limiting device or ballast. Automotive supplies are notoriously noise-prone, therefore adequate transient protection should be used to prevent damage to the semiconductors. The high frequency inverter may also be used to operate fluorescent lighting from stand-by batteries for emergency lighting applications where mains failure may occur.

# Non-maintained emergency lighting

The lamp is only lit when the mains supply falls below a pre-set minimum level. During normal mains conditions, the nickel-cadmium batteries are charged via R4. The LED indicates that battery charging is in progress. During normal mains conditions TR1 is turned on via ZD1 and R2 and consequently TR2 is held in the off-state thereby interrupting the supply to the inverter TR3 and TR4. When the mains supply falls such that ZD1 no longer conducts, TR2 is turned on and the inverter is energized thereby lighting the lamp. Over three hours of emergency light is then provided.

### Electronic transformer

The 12V tungsten-halogen lamp may be powered by a 50Hz step-down transformer however with lamp wattages of 75W, the transformer starts to become bulky. The electronic transformer is a lightweight solution to supplying power to tungsten-halogen lamps which lends itself to integration with the lamp fitting. The mains supply is full-wave rectified and then inverted at approximately 30kHz. The step-down transformer is then a light-weight small-size ferrite cored device. The BR100 diac "kick-starts" the inverter at power-up and D1 disables the "kick-start" when the inverter is running.

### Ignitor

Sodium discharge lamps may not be connected directly to the mains supply as the current through the gas discharge must be limited. This is traditionally accomplished by an inductor called a ballast. The lamp will not start however, when the mains is connected and a means of ignition is required; this is termed an ignitor. An ignitor is an electronic circuit which interacts with the ballast to produce high voltage pulses in the order of 1.8 to 5kV depending upon the lamp to be ignited. The ballast is usually provided with a tap which enables the ignitor to supply pulses of current through part of the ballast's winding. The ballast acts as a step-up auto-transformer generating the high voltage striking pulses across the lamp. A typical ignitor circuit is shown below.

When power is first applied, the lamp is not struck and the voltage across the lamp is the mains supply. This is potentially divided by R3 and R4 and the diac conducts causing the triac to be triggered into pulsed conduction via C1 around the peak of each half cycle of the mains supply. An ignition pulse is produced each time the triac conducts. When the lamp is struck, the running voltage is lower than the mains supply and the diac ceases to conduct; the ignitor is then disabled.

# 9 Heat

### Temperature co-efficients

All electronic components change in value and performance with changes in temperature. The circuit designer must be aware of these changes and allow or compensate for them in the design. In general, semiconductor parameters increase with temperature. This is not always desirable. The gain of a transistor increases with temperature which may improve a circuit's performance but the collector to base leakage current also increases with temperature which can degrade the performance.

### Thermal management

Some electronic components generate heat during their operation. If the heat is of a low order, the component's body and connecting leads may be able to dissipate the heat and not cause the component's temperature to rise above the manufacturer's specified maximum limit. If the heat is such that the component's temperature exceeds the maximum then, assuming the design cannot be electronically modified, the heat must be extracted at a faster rate by either improving ventilation or heat-sinking the component.

### Appreciation of temperature

The electronics engineer should have a "feel" for temperature levels which occur in electronics and related subjects. The first instinct is to touch the component to estimate its temperature and the "engineer's finger test" is used by many electronics engineers. It should be stressed however that extreme caution should be exercised when using the engineer's finger test. The component being touched may exceed 100°C in which case injury may be sustained. Even worse, the component could be live.

The table shown overleaf details some common temperatures which occur in engineering.

## ENGINEER'S FINGER TEST  (°C)

| | | | |
|---|---|---|---|
| Skin sticks | -20° or below | Can hold finger on for seconds | 60°C |
| Cool can of beer | 4°C | Can hold finger on for 1 sec. * | 70°C |
| Barely getting warm | 30°C | Can hold finger on < 1 sec | 80°C |
| Finger temperature | 37°C | Finger is withdrawn quickly | 90+°C |
| Getting warm | 40°C | Blister (not recommended) | 120+°C |
| Can hold palm on indefinitely | 50°C | | |

\* Mnemonic 1 SEcond is SEventy degrees

# Temperature reference chart

| CATEGORY | DESCRIPTION | °CELSIUS | °FAHRENHEIT |
|---|---|---|---|
| **Electronics** | Maximum silicon junction temperature<br>60/40 solder melts | 150 to 175<br>188 | 302 to 347<br>370.4 |
| **Physics** | Water freezes<br>Water boils | 0<br>100 | 32<br>212 |
| **Melting point of metals** | Mercury<br>Sodium<br>Tin<br>Lead<br>Zinc<br>Magnesium<br>Aluminium<br>Silver<br>Gold<br>Copper<br>Nickel<br>Iron<br>Platinum<br>Tungsten | -39<br>98<br>232<br>327<br>419<br>659<br>660<br>961<br>1063<br>1083<br>1455<br>1527<br>1773<br>3387 | -38.2<br>208.4<br>449.6<br>620.6<br>786.2<br>1218.2<br>1220.0<br>1761.8<br>1945.4<br>1981.4<br>2651.0<br>2780.6<br>3223.4<br>6128.6 |
| **Plastics** | PVC max<br>EVA max<br>PTFE Max<br>Silicone rubber<br>Natural rubber | 100<br>140<br>250<br>150<br>60 | 212<br>284<br>482<br>302<br>140 |
| **Domestic** | Home freezer<br>Home fridge<br>Feels chilly<br>Comfortable room temperature<br>Feels far too hot<br>Body temperature | -18<br>4<br>10<br>25<br>35<br>36.9 | 0<br>39.2<br>50<br>77<br>95<br>98.4 |

**To convert °C to °F multiply by 9/5 and add 32**
**To convert °F to °C  subtract 32 and multiply by 5/9**
**To convert K to °C subtract 273**

# Temperature coefficients (passive)

**Resistors**

| TYPE | ppm / °C |
|------|----------|
| Carbon Composition | +200 to -2000 |
| Carbon Film | +200 to -1000 |
| Metal Film | ±50 |
| Metal Oxide | ±200 |
| Metal Glaze | ±200 |
| Wirewound | ±100 to ±200 |
| Surface Mount | ±200 |

**Film capacitors**

| TYPE | ppm / °C (0 to 80°C) |
|------|----------------------|
| Polyester Film & Foil | +500 |
| Metallized Polyester | +400 |
| Polypropylene Film / Foil | -200 |
| Metallized Polypropylene | -300 |
| Polycarbonate Film/Foil | -25 |
| Metallized Polycarbonate | -25 |
| Polystyrene | -60 |
| | |

# Temperature coefficients (active)

## Bipolar transistors

All temperature drift effects cause the collector current to rise with temperature.

| | |
|---|---|
| $V_{be}$ | -2.5 mV/ °C |
| $h_{FE}$ | +2% / °C |
| $I_{CBO}$ | doubles for every 10 °C rise |

## N channel MOSFETs

| | |
|---|---|
| $V_{gs(th)}$ | -5 mV/ °C |
| $g_{fs}$ | -0.2% / °C |
| $R_{DS (on)}$ | doubles for every 100 °C rise |
| Switching Times | Independent of temp |

## Thyristors and triacs

| | |
|---|---|
| $I_{GT}$ | Reduces by 10% for every 10 °C rise |
| $I_{holding}$ | Reduces by 5 % for every 10 °C rise |
| $I_{latching}$ | Reduces by 10% for every 10 °C rise |

## Zener diodes (400mW)

| ZENER VOLTAGE | TEMP COEFFICIENT |
|---|---|
| 2.7V | -3 mV/°C |
| 4.7V | -2 mV/°C |
| 5.6V | approx 0mV/°C |
| 9.1V | +5mV/°C |
| 15V | +11mV/°C |
| 30V | +27mV/°C |
| 75V | +80mV/°C |

# Thermal impedance calculations

### Semiconductors

Semiconductor devices are fabricated on a small piece of semiconductor material (such as silicon) which is commonly called a chip. The chip is mounted inside a package which may be plastic or metal. When the device generates power, heat is produced. The heat flows through the packaging material and if the package is not in thermal contact with another object, the heat will radiate from the outside of the package to the surroundings. As the heat flows through the package, and radiates to the surroundings, a temperature gradient is produced. The chip's temperature is therefore higher than the surroundings by an amount that is proportional to the power in the chip. The temperature rise of the chip above the surroundings per watt in the chip is called the thermal impedance of the package and is given in degrees Celsius or Kelvin per watt.

An electrical equivalent circuit may be devised to calculate the thermal conditions of the device. The power in the chip may be represented by a current source. The thermal impedance of the device may be represented by a resistor, and the temperature rise of the chip represented by the voltage produced across the resistor by the current source.

ELECTRICAL EQUIVALENT CIRCUIT TO THE THERMAL CIRCUIT OF A DEVICE

The temperature of the chip is therefore the temperature of the surroundings plus the temperature rise across the thermal impedance of the package. Traditionally, thermal impedances were quoted for transistors and therefore the term **junction** is used rather than chip.

The symbol used for thermal impedance is the Greek letter theta $\theta$.
The symbol representing the total thermal impedance of the package of a device, from its chip (or junction) to the surroundings, is denoted: $\theta_{\text{junc-ambient}}$ or simply $\theta_{\text{j-a}}$.

---

**The temperature of the chip = Ambient temp + $P \cdot \theta_{\text{j-a}}$**

---

(Where **P** = power in the chip in watts.)

## Heat sinks

The temperature of the chip or junction must not be allowed to exceed a maximum which for silicon is typically 150 degrees Celsius. Manufacturers denote the maxiumum temperature of the chip in a device by the symbol $T_j$ . If the calculation shown on the previous page is carried out and shows that the chip's temperature will exceed its maximum $T_j$ then, if it is not possible to reduce the power in the chip or reduce the ambient temperature, the device must be mounted on a heat sink. Heat will flow into the heat sink and will then radiate to the surroundings from the greater surface area of the heat sink. The heat sink will have a thermal impedance which quantifies the temperature rise of the heat sink above the surroundings for a given power in the device. This may be given the symbol $\theta_{HS}$.

It may be necessary to electrically insulate the device from the heat sink and the insulator will also have a thermal impedance $\theta_{INS}$ . The manufacturer of the device will quote a second thermal impedance which represents the temperature rise from the junction (chip) to the outside case of the package. This is given the symbol $\theta_{j-c}$ ( $\theta_{junction-case}$ ).

An electrical equivalent circuit may be devised to enable the chip's temperature to be calculated.

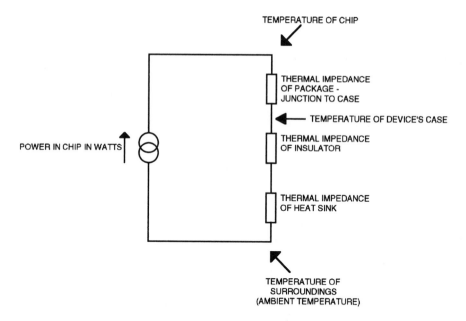

THE ELECTRICAL EQUIVALENT CIRCUIT WHEN THE DEVICE IS CONNECTED TO A HEAT SINK

The temperature of the chip $\quad$ = Ambient temp $\quad + \quad P\ (\ \theta_{j-c} + \theta_{INS} + \theta_{HS}\ )$

# Thermal impedances of semiconductor packages - plastic

| CASE OUTLINE | $\theta$ junc-free air °C /W | $\theta$ junc-case °C /W | $\theta$ case-heat sink Without insulator °C /W | | $\theta$ case-heat sink With insulator °C /W | |
|---|---|---|---|---|---|---|
| | | | No heat sink compound | With heat sink compound | No heat sink compound | With heat sink compound |
| TO92 | 200 to 357 | 60 | - | - | - | - |
| TO126 | 83.3 to 100 | 3.3 to 10 | | | | |
| TO220 | 62 to 70 | 1.5 to 4.2 | 1.2 to 2 | 0.6 to 1.2 | | 2.1 to 2.6 |
| TO202 | 62.5 to 75 | 7.5 to 12.5 | | | | |
| TO218 | 35.7 | 1 to 1.56 | | | | 0.6 |

# Thermal impedances of semiconductor packages - metal

| CASE OUTLINE | $\theta$ junc-free air °C /W | $\theta$ junc-case °C /W | $\theta$ case-heat sink Without insulator °C /W | | $\theta$ case-heat sink With insulator °C /W | |
|---|---|---|---|---|---|---|
| | | | No heat sink compound | With heat sink compound | No heat sink compound | With heat sink compound |
| TO18 | 500 | 150 to 200 | | | | |
| TO39 | 175 to 190 | 25 to 40 | | | | |
| TO3 | 32 to 43 | 1 | 0.05 to 0.2 | 0.005 to 0.1 | 0.55 to 0.8 | 0.28 to 0.4 |

# Thermocouples

### *Definition*

A thermocouple is two dissimilar metal wires joined at each end to form an electrical circuit. If the two junctions are at different temperatures, a voltage is produced between the wires due to the Seebeck effect.

Metal A

**Junction**     **Junction**

Metal B

A THERMOCOUPLE

### *Background*

The number of free electrons in a metal is dependent upon its type and its temperature. If two dissimilar metal wires are joined together at each end a small voltage exists between them. If the junctions are at the same temperature then no current will flow as the same voltage exists at each junction and one voltage exactly opposes the other. When the junctions are at different temperatures, the voltages are different and with some combinations of metals, the difference in voltages is almost proportional to the temperature difference. When an attempt is made to measure the voltage difference with a voltmeter by breaking into the circuit, other thermocouples are formed when the wires of the voltmeter are connected to the metal wires. If these new junctions are both kept at the same temperature however, the voltages produced will be equal and will cancel each other out. The voltmeter will therefore indicate the temperature difference between the two main junctions. An engineer may wish to measure the temperature of an object such as a transistor and one of the junctions of the thermocouple will be attached to the transistor. This junction is usually referred to as the **hot junction** If the other junction (referred to as the **cold junction**) is at room temperature then the voltmeter will simply indicate the temperature difference between the transistor and the room. For the voltmeter to read the absolute temperature of the transistor in degrees Celsius, it is necessary to allow for the temperature of the cold junction. This is termed **cold junction compensation.**

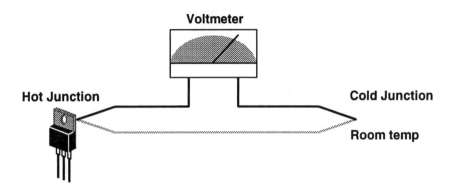

**Voltmeter**

**Hot Junction**     **Cold Junction**

**Room temp**

### Cold junction compensation

The cold junction is maintained at 0 degrees Celsius by immersing in melting ice. The hot junction will then read directly in degrees Celsius.

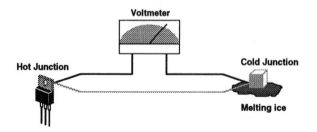

### Practical

A semiconductor  sensor is used to measure the temperature of the cold junction.  It generates a voltage which is equal and opposite to the voltage produced by the cold junction.  The voltmeter therefore indicates the temperature of the hot junction in degrees Celsius.

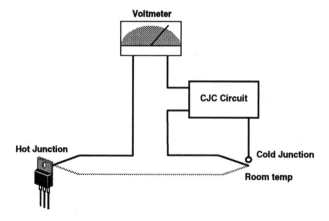

### Thermocouple conditioning IC

A semiconductor manufacturer called Analogue Devices has made life very easy by incorporating all the necessary conditioning circuits on one integrated circuit.  The circuit is suitable for a type K thermocouple and gives an output of 10mV per degree Celsius.  The circuit is suitable for recording temperatures of from -180 to 1100 degrees Celsius.

**Thermocouple data**

| ANSI | JUNCTION MATERIALS | ALTERNATIVE NAMES | INSULATION COLOURS | SHEATH COLOUR | TEMP RANGE | TOTAL O/P OVER RANGE | APPROX uV/°C AT 100 °C |
|------|--------------------|--------------------|--------------------|---------------|------------|----------------------|------------------------|
| B | + Platinum - 30% Rhodium <br> - Platinum - 6% Rhodium | | | - | 100 to 1600 °C | 13.6 mV | 1 uV/°C |
| E | + Nickel Chromium <br> - Copper - Nickel | Chromel <br> Constantan | Brown <br> Blue | Brown | 0 to 800 °C | 75 mV | 68 uV/°C |
| J | + Iron <br> - Copper - Nickel | Constantan | Yellow <br> Blue | Black | -180 to 700 °C | 50 mV | 46 uV/°C |
| K | + Nickel Chromium <br> - Nickel - Aluminium | Chromel <br> Alumel | Brown <br> Blue | Red | -180 to 1100 °C | 56 mV | 42 uV/°C |
| R | + Platinum - 13% Rhodium <br> - Platinum | | White <br> Blue | Green | 0 to 1600 °C | 18.7 mV | 8 uV/°C |
| S | + Platinum - 10% Rhodium <br> - Platinum | | White <br> Blue | Green | 0 to 1550 °C | 16 mV | 8 uV/°C |
| T | + Copper <br> - Copper - Nickel | Constantan | White <br> Blue | Blue | -185 to 300 °C | 26 mV | 46 uV/°C |

Source - BS4937,1843

**Semiconductor temperature sensor**

The AD590 is a current source device which gives 1uA per Kelvin. It is suitable for the range -50 to +150 degrees Celsius. When the device is at 0 degrees Celsius it outputs a nominal 273 uA. This must be allowed for if a reading in degrees C is required. A suitable circuit to convert the AD590 output to 10mV per degree C is shown below. RV1 is adjusted to give 2.73V at the output of IC1. RV2 is adjusted so that the output of IC2 gives 10mV per Kelvin. The voltage difference between the two op-amp outputs is therefore 10mV per degree Celsius.

**AD590 conditioning circuit**

The circuit serves as a useful device to convert a standard digital multimeter to a digital thermometer. The AD590 may be fitted as a probe tip.

# 10 Connections

## Integrated circuit pin-outs
### Dual in-line integrated circuits

**TOP VIEWS**

HOLD "CUT-OUT" TO LEFT

DOT DENOTES PIN 1

PIN NUMBERS
INCREASE ANTI-CLOCKWISE

---

**Metal package**

**TOP VIEW**

- Highest numbered pin is always next to tab.
- Pins are numbered anticlockwise.
- A metal package may be inserted into a dual in-line position by arranging the pins into two rows.

---

### Single in-line integrated circuits

The pins are numbered from left to right looking at the IC legend.

## RS232C

RS232C is a serial communication system or standard which was originally developed to enable computer terminals to communicate with modems. It has gradually evolved into a common serial communication system between computers and peripherals such as printers (or even other computers).

The original system used nine or more wires between the computer terminal DTE (data terminal equipment) and the modem DCE (data circuit termination equipment). Many of the wires were used in a "handshake" routine between the computer and the modem. The main wires which carry the data are TXD (transmit data), RXD (receive data) and common or 0V. Modern systems use a software "handshake" called Xon Xoff protocol and in these cases only the 3 main wires TXD, RXD and 0V are required between the two items of equipment.

The most popular type of connector which is used for the RS232C system is the 25 way 'D' connector.

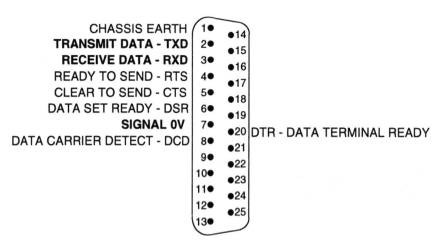

25 WAY "D" CONNECTOR
LOOKING AT SOLDER CONNECTIONS

### Making an RS232C connection between computer and peripheral

If there is software Xon Xoff protocol used by the equipment, then the simple connection below may work.

If the above does not work, the "hardware handshake" at the computer may have to be defeated as below.

If the above does not work, the peripheral may require a DTR and RTS signal as below.

### Making an RS232C connection between computers

When two computers are connected, the TXD and RXD connections have to be mirrored. Some peripherals may also need this mirrored connection. If there are no hardware handshaking requirements to satisfy, the connection arrangement below may work.

If there are hardware handshaking requirements, they may be defeated as below.

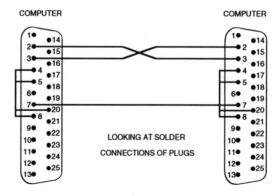

The RS232C system is such that if an error is made during interconnection, no damage will occur to the equipment.

# Audio connections
## 5 pin DIN

**DIN PLUG LOOKING AT SOLDER CONNECTIONS**

| | LEFT LINE I/P (RECORD) | RIGHT LINE I/P (RECORD) | 0V | RIGHT LINE O/P (PLAY) | LEFT LINE O/P (PLAY) |
|---|---|---|---|---|---|
| **STEREO TAPE RECORDER** | LEFT LINE I/P (RECORD) | RIGHT LINE I/P (RECORD) | 0V | RIGHT LINE O/P (PLAY) | LEFT LINE O/P (PLAY) |
| **MONO TAPE RECORDER** | LINE I/P (RECORD) | | 0V | | LINE O/P (PLAY) |
| **STEREO MICROPHONE UNBALANCED** | LEFT | RIGHT | 0V | | |
| **STEREO MICROPHONE BALANCED** | LEFT + | RIGHT + | 0V | RIGHT - | LEFT - |
| **VINYL RECORD PICK-UP** | | | LEFT 0V BLUE RT 0V GREEN | RIGHT SIGNAL (RED) | LEFT SIGNAL (WHITE) |

FOR A 5 PIN DIN AMPLIFIER CONNECTION, LEFT LINE I/P BECOMES LEFT LINE O/P ETC.

## 3 Pin XLR Plug

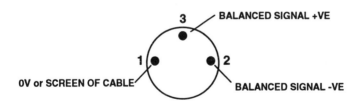

**MALE PLUG  LOOKING AT SOLDER CONNECTIONS**

3 — BALANCED SIGNAL +VE

1 — 0V or SCREEN OF CABLE

2 — BALANCED SIGNAL -VE

## Thermionic valve pin-outs

Thermionic valves are still used today in musical instrument amplifiers as manufactured by companies such as Marshall. There are a limited number of types used today and they are shown below.

### Pre-amp valves ECC81, 82, 83(dual triode)

Heater voltage (each side) = 6.3V rms
Typical anode voltage when used in class A =150V dc

**ECC81 = 12AT7 = 6201**
**ECC82 = 12AU7 = 7730**
**ECC83 = 12AX7 = 7025**

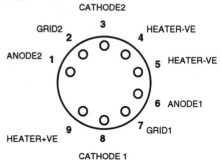

**UNDERSIDE VIEW**
**LOOKING AT SOLDER PINS**

### Output valve, EL34 pentode

For two valves in push-pull
Anode quiescent current = 30mA
Grid 1 (control grid) bias = -33V
Grid 2 (screen grid) voltage is usually same as anode
Grid 3 (suppressor grid) voltage = 0V
Heater voltage 6.3V rms

**EL34**

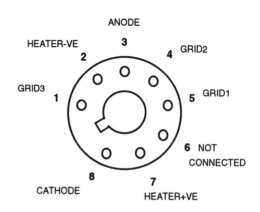

**UNDERSIDE VIEW**
**LOOKING AT SOLDER PINS**

**Output valve, EL84 pentode**
For two valves in push-pull
Anode quiescent current = 30mA
Grid 2 (screen grid) voltage is usually same as anode
Grid 3 connected to cathode
Heater voltage 6.3V rms (760mA)

ANODE

GRID3
GRID1
2
9 GRID2

3 4 5
CATHODE
HEATER

**EL84**

CATHODE & GRID 3

GRID1 3
2

NOT CONNECTED 1

HEATER
4

5 HEATER

6 NOT CONNECTED

GRID2 9

8 7 ANODE

NOT CONNECTED

**UNDERSIDE VIEW
LOOKING AT SOLDER PINS**

# 21 pin SCART plug

All designations are with respect to the appliance the plug is inserted into
e.g. If plugged into a tv the "audio output" means an audio signal from the tv.

**VIEW OF PLUG FROM THE WIRING SIDE**

| | |
|---|---|
| AUDIO INPUT (RIGHT) 2 | 1 AUDIO OUTPUT (RIGHT) |
| AUDIO GROUND 4 | 3 AUDIO OUTPUT (LEFT) |
| AUDIO INPUT (LEFT) 6 | 5 BLUE GROUND |
| AV MODE (12V, 10k) 8 | 7 BLUE INPUT |
| INTERCOM DATA 10 | 9 GREEN GROUND |
| INTERCOM DATA 12 | 11 GREEN INPUT |
| INTERCOM DATA 14 | 13 RED GROUND |
| BLANKING (3V, 75 OHM) 16 | 15 RED INPUT |
| BLANKING GROUND 18 | 17 VIDEO GROUND |
| VIDEO/ SYNC INPUT 20 | 19 VIDEO OUTPUT |

**PIN 21 IS THE METAL SHIELD OF THE PLUG**

# Appendix
**Decimal prefixes**

| POWER OF 10 | PREFIX | PREFIX LETTER |
|:---:|:---:|:---:|
| $10^{18}$ | exa | E |
| $10^{15}$ | peta | P |
| $10^{12}$ | tera | T |
| $10^9$ | giga | G |
| $10^6$ | mega | M |
| $10^3$ | kilo | k |
| $10^2$ | hecto | h |
| 10 | deca | da |
| $10^{-1}$ | deci | d |
| $10^{-2}$ | centi | c |
| $10^{-3}$ | milli | m |
| $10^{-6}$ | micro | $\mu$ |
| $10^{-9}$ | nano | n |
| $10^{-12}$ | pico | p |
| $10^{-15}$ | femto | f |
| $10^{-18}$ | atto | A |

# Greek alphabet

The Greek alphabet has 24 letters and some are used to denote certain parameters in electronic engineering.

| NAME | LOWER CASE | DESIGNATION OF LOWER CASE | UPPER CASE | DESIGNATION OF UPPER CASE |
|------|-----------|--------------------------|-----------|--------------------------|
| ALPHA | α | COMMON BASE CURRENT GAIN | A | |
| BETA | β | COMMON EMITTER CURR GAIN | B | |
| GAMMA | γ | | Γ | |
| DELTA | δ | PARTIAL DERIVATIVE | Δ | A SMALL CHANGE |
| EPSILON | ε | PERMITTIVITY | E | |
| ZETA | ζ | DAMPING RATIO | Z | |
| ETA | η | EFFICIENCY | H | |
| THETA | θ | ANGLE | Θ | |
| IOTA | ι | | I | |
| KAPPA | κ | | K | |
| LAMBDA | λ | WAVELENGTH, FLUX LINKAGE | Λ | |
| MU | μ | 1 MILLIONTH,    PERMEABILITY | M | |
| NU | ν | | N | |
| XI | ξ | | Ξ | |
| OMIKRON | o | | O | |
| PI | π | RATIO  CIRCUMF TO DIAMETER | Π | |
| RHO | ρ | RESISTIVITY,  CHARGE DENSITY | P | |
| SIGMA | σ | CONDUCTIVITY | Σ | THE SUM OF... |
| TAU | τ | TIME CONSTANT | T | |
| UPSILON | υ | | Y | |
| PHI | φ | PHASE ANGLE, MAGNETIC FLUX | Φ | |
| CHI | χ | | X | |
| PSI | ψ | ANGLE, ELECTRIC FLUX | Ψ | |
| OMEGA | ω | ANGULAR FREQUENCY RADIANS/SEC | Ω | OHMS |

# Delta-star, star-delta transformations

### Delta-star transformation

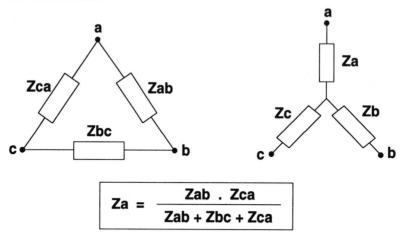

$$Za = \frac{Zab \cdot Zca}{Zab + Zbc + Zca}$$

The star impedance is equal to the product of the two impedances at the node divided by the sum of the impedances.

### Star-delta transformation

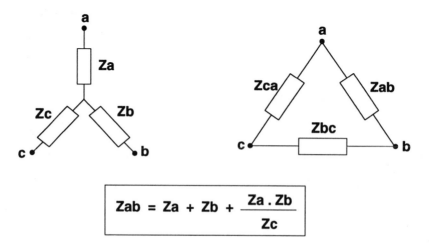

$$Zab = Za + Zb + \frac{Za \cdot Zb}{Zc}$$

Add the two impedances between the points then add their product divided by the third impedance.

# Physical constants

| CONSTANT | SYMBOL | VALUE | UNITS |
|---|---|---|---|
| AVOGADRO'S NO | N | $6.023 \times 10^{26}$ | /KG MOLE |
| ACCELERATION OF GRAVITY | g | 9.807 | METRES / SEC$^2$ |
| BOHR MAGNETRON | $\beta$ | $9.27 \times 10^{-25}$ | AMPS / M$^2$ |
| BOLTZMANN'S CONSTANT | k | $1.38 \times 10^{-23}$ | JOULES / $^\circ$K |
| CHARACTERISTIC Z OF FREE SPACE | $Z_o = (\mu_o / \varepsilon_o)^{-1/2}$ | $120 \pi$ | OHMS |
| ELECTRON - VOLT | eV | $1.602 \times 10^{-19}$ | JOULES |
| ELECTRON CHARGE | e | $1.602 \times 10^{-19}$ | COULOMBS |
| ELECTRON REST MASS | $m_e$ | $9.109 \times 10^{-31}$ | KILOGRAMS |
| ELECTRON CHARGE / MASS RATIO | | $1.759 \times 10^{11}$ | COULOMBS / KG |
| ENERGY FOR T = 290 $^\circ$K | kT | $4 \times 10^{-21}$ | JOULES |
| ENERGY OF GROUND STATE ATOM | | 13.6 | ELECTRON - V |
| FARADAY CONSTANT | F | $9.65 \times 10^{7}$ | C / KG - MOLE |
| MECHANICAL EQUIVALENT OF HEAT | | 4.1855 | JOULES/CAL |
| PERMEABILITY OF FREE SPACE | $\mu_o$ | $4 \pi \times 10^{-7}$ | HENRIES / M |
| PERMITTIVITY OF FREE SPACE | $\varepsilon_o$ | $1/36\pi \times 10^{-9}$ | FARADS / M |
| PLANCK'S CONSTANT | h | $6.626 \times 10^{-34}$ | JOULE - SECS |
| PROTON MASS | $m_p$ | $1.672 \times 10^{-27}$ | KILOGRAMS |
| PROTON / ELECTRON MASS RATIO | | 1836.1 | |
| STEFAN - BOLTZMANN CONSTANT | $\sigma$ | $1.672 \times 10^{-27}$ | |
| UNIVERSAL GAS CONSTANT | R | 8.314 | KJ/KG MOLE $^\circ$K |
| VELOCITY OF LIGHT IN A VACUUM | c | $2.998 \times 10^{8}$ | METRES /SEC |
| VELOCITY OF SOUND IN AIR @ SEA LV | | 1100 | FT / SECOND |
| VOLUME OF 1KG MOLE OF GAS@NTP | | 22.42 | CUBIC METRES |

# UNITS CONVERSION CHART - LENGTH

| | ANG-STROM | MICRO-METRE | MILLI-METRE | CENTI-METRE | INCH | FOOT (ft) | YARD (yds) | METRE (m) | FATHOM | KILO-METRE | MILE | UK NAUT. MILE |
|---|---|---|---|---|---|---|---|---|---|---|---|---|
| ANG-STROM | 1 | 0,0001 | 1,000E-07 | 1,000E-08 | 3,937E-09 | 3,281E-10 | 1,094E-10 | 1,00E-10 | 5,468E-11 | 1,000E-13 | 6,214E-14 | 5,397E-14 |
| MICRO-METRE | 10000 | 1 | 1,000E-03 | 1,000E-04 | 3,937E-05 | 3,281E-06 | 1,094E-06 | 1,00E-06 | 5,468E-07 | 1,000E-09 | 6,214E-10 | 5,397E-10 |
| MILLI-METRE | 1,000E+07 | 1000 | 1 | 0,1 | 3,937E-02 | 3,281E-03 | 1,094E-03 | 0,0010 | 5,468E-04 | 1,000E-06 | 6,214E-07 | 5,397E-07 |
| CENTI-METRE | 1,000E+08 | 1,000E+04 | 10 | 1 | 0,3937 | 3,281E-02 | 1,094E-02 | 0,0100 | 5,468E-03 | 1,000E-05 | 6,214E-06 | 5,397E-06 |
| INCH | 2,540E+08 | 2,540E+04 | 25,4 | 2,54 | 1 | 8,333E-02 | 2,778E-02 | 0,0254 | 1,389E-02 | 2,540E-05 | 1,578E-05 | 1,371E-05 |
| FOOT (ft) | 3,048E+09 | 3,048E+05 | 304,8 | 30,48 | 12 | 1 | 0,3333 | 0,3048 | 0,1667 | 3,048E-04 | 1,894E-04 | 1,645E-04 |
| YARD (yds) | 9,144E+09 | 9,144E+05 | 914,4 | 91,44 | 36 | 3 | 1 | 0,9144 | 0,5 | 9,144E-04 | 5,682E-04 | 4,935E-04 |
| METRE (m) | 1,000E+10 | 1,000E+06 | 1,000E+03 | 100 | 39,37 | 3,281 | 1,094 | 1 | 0,5468 | 1,000E-03 | 6,214E-04 | 5,397E-04 |
| FATHOM | 1,829E+10 | 1,829E+06 | 1,829E+03 | 182,9 | 72,01 | 6,001 | 2 | 1,829 | 1 | 1,829E-03 | 1,136E-03 | 9,869E-04 |
| KILO-METRE | 1,000E+13 | 1,000E+09 | 1,000E+06 | 100000 | 39370 | 3281 | 1094 | 1000 | 546,8 | 1 | 0,6214 | 0,5397 |
| MILE | 1,609E+13 | 1,609E+09 | 1,609E+06 | 160934 | 63360 | 5280 | 1760 | 1609 | 880,0 | 1,609 | 1 | 0,8685 |
| UK NAUT. MILE | 1,853E+13 | 1,853E+09 | 1,853E+06 | 185318 | 72960 | 6080 | 2027 | 1853 | 1013 | 1,853 | 1,152 | 1 |

# UNITS CONVERSION CHART - VOLUME

| | CUBIC mm | MILLI-LITRES | CUBIC INCHES | UK FLUID OUNCE | US FLUID OUNCE | US PINT | UK PINT | LITRE | US GALLON | UK GALLON | CUBIC FEET | CUBIC YARDS | CUBIC METRES |
|---|---|---|---|---|---|---|---|---|---|---|---|---|---|
| CUBIC mm | 1 | 0,001 | 6,102E-05 | 3,520E-05 | 3,381E-05 | 2,113E-06 | 1,760E-06 | 1,000E-06 | 2,642E-07 | 2,200E-07 | 3,531E-08 | 1,308E-09 | 1,000E-09 |
| MILLI-LITRES | 1000 | 1 | 6,102E-02 | 3,520E-02 | 3,381E-02 | 2,113E-03 | 1,760E-03 | 1,000E-03 | 2,642E-04 | 2,200E-04 | 3,531E-05 | 1,308E-06 | 1,000E-06 |
| CUBIC INCHES | 16387 | 16,387 | 1 | 0,5767 | 0,5541 | 3,463E-02 | 2,884E-02 | 1,639E-02 | 4,329E-03 | 3,605E-03 | 5,787E-04 | 2,143E-05 | 1,639E-05 |
| UK FLUID OUNCE | 2,841E+04 | 28,41 | 1,734 | 1 | 0,9607 | 6,004E-02 | 4,999E-02 | 2,841E-02 | 7,505E-03 | 6,249E-03 | 1,003E-03 | 3,716E-05 | 2,841E-05 |
| US FLUID OUNCE | 2,957E+04 | 29,57 | 1,804 | 1,041 | 1 | 6,249E-02 | 5,204E-02 | 2,957E-02 | 7,812E-03 | 6,504E-03 | 1,044E-03 | 3,868E-05 | 2,957E-05 |
| US PINT | 4,732E+05 | 473,18 | 28,88 | 16,65 | 16 | 1 | 0,8327 | 0,4732 | 0,1250 | 0,1041 | 1,671E-02 | 6,189E-04 | 4,732E-04 |
| UK PINT | 5,683E+05 | 568,3 | 34,68 | 20 | 19,22 | 1,201 | 1 | 0,5683 | 0,1501 | 0,1250 | 2,007E-02 | 7,433E-04 | 5,683E-04 |
| LITRE | 1,000E+06 | 1000 | 61,02 | 35,20 | 33,81 | 2,113 | 1,760 | 1 | 0,2642 | 0,2200 | 3,531E-02 | 1,308E-03 | 1,000E-03 |
| US GALLON | 3,785E+06 | 3785,4 | 231,0 | 133,2 | 128 | 8 | 6,661 | 3,785 | 1 | 0,8327 | 0,1337 | 4,951E-03 | 3,785E-03 |
| UK GALLON | 4,546E+06 | 4546,1 | 277,4 | 160 | 154 | 9,608 | 8 | 4,546 | 1,201 | 1 | 0,1605 | 5,946E-03 | 4,546E-03 |
| CUBIC FEET | 2,832E+07 | 28320 | 1728 | 996,7 | 958 | 59,85 | 49,84 | 28,32 | 7,481 | 6,230 | 1 | 3,704E-02 | 2,832E-02 |
| CUBIC YARDS | 7,646E+08 | 764559 | 46656 | 26909 | 25853 | 1616 | 1345 | 764,6 | 202 | 168,2 | 27 | 1 | 0,7646 |
| CUBIC METRES | 1,000E+09 | 1,000E+06 | 61024 | 35195 | 33814 | 2113 | 1760 | 1000 | 264,2 | 220 | 35,31 | 1,308 | 1 |

# UNITS CONVERSION CHART - VELOCITY

| FEET PER MINUTE | CM/SEC | METRES/ MINUTE | INCHES/ SECOND | KMETRES/ HOUR | FEET/ SECOND | MILES/ HOUR | METRES/ SECOND |
|---|---|---|---|---|---|---|---|
| 1 | 0,50800001 | 0,3048 | 0,2 | 1,829E-02 | 1,667E-02 | 1,136E-02 | 5,08E-03 |
| 1,969 | 1 | 0,6 | 0,3937 | 3,600E-02 | 3,281E-02 | 2,237E-02 | 0,01 |
| 3,281 | 1,667 | 1 | 0,6562 | 0,06 | 5,468E-02 | 3,728E-02 | 1,67E-02 |
| 5 | 2,54 | 1,524E+00 | 1 | 9,144E-02 | 8,333E-02 | 5,682E-02 | 2,54E-02 |
| 54,68 | 27,78 | 16,67 | 10,94 | 1 | 0,9113 | 0,6214 | 0,2778 |
| 60 | 30,48 | 18,29 | 12 | 1,097 | 1 | 0,6818 | 0,3048 |
| 88 | 44,70 | 26,82 | 17,60 | 1,609 | 1,467 | 1 | 0,447 |
| 196,9 | 100 | 60 | 39,37 | 3,6 | 3,281 | 2,237 | 1 |

# UNITS CONVERSION CHART - MASS

| | MICRO-GRAM | MILLI-GRAM | GRAM | OUNCE | POUND | KILO-GRAM | STONE | SLUG | HUNDRED WEIGHT | METRIC TONNE | UK TON |
|---|---|---|---|---|---|---|---|---|---|---|---|
| MICRO-GRAM | 1 | 0,001 | 1,000E-06 | 3,527E-08 | 2,205E-09 | 1,000E-09 | 1,575E-10 | 6,853E-11 | 1,968E-11 | 1,000E-12 | 9,854E-13 |
| MILLI-GRAM | 1000 | 1 | 1,000E-03 | 3,527E-05 | 2,205E-06 | 1,000E-06 | 1,575E-07 | 6,853E-08 | 1,968E-08 | 1,000E-09 | 9,854E-10 |
| GRAM | 1,000E+06 | 1000 | 1 | 3,527E-02 | 2,205E-03 | 1,000E-03 | 1,575E-04 | 6,853E-05 | 1,968E-05 | 1,000E-06 | 9,854E-07 |
| OUNCE | 2,835E+07 | 2,835E+04 | 2,835E+01 | 1 | 6,250E-02 | 2,835E-02 | 4,464E-03 | 1,943E-03 | 5,580E-04 | 2,836E-05 | 2,794E-05 |
| POUND | 4,536E+08 | 4,536E+05 | 4,536E+02 | 1,600E+01 | 1 | 4,536E-01 | 7,143E-02 | 3,108E-02 | 8,929E-03 | 4,537E-04 | 4,470E-04 |
| KILO-GRAM | 1,000E+09 | 1,000E+06 | 1,000E+03 | 3,527E+01 | 2,205E+00 | 1 | 1,575E-01 | 6,853E-02 | 1,968E-02 | 1,000E-03 | 9,854E-04 |
| STONE | 6,350E+09 | 6,350E+06 | 6,350E+03 | 2,240E+02 | 1,400E+01 | 6,350E+00 | 1 | 4,352E-01 | 1,250E-01 | 6,352E-03 | 6,258E-03 |
| SLUG | 1,466E+10 | 1,466E+07 | 1,466E+04 | 5,171E+02 | 3,232E+01 | 1,466E+01 | 2,309E+00 | 1 | 2,886E-01 | 1,466E-02 | 1,445E-02 |
| HUNDRED WEIGHT | 5,080E+10 | 5,080E+07 | 5,080E+04 | 1,792E+03 | 1,120E+02 | 5,080E+01 | 8,000E+00 | 3,481E+00 | 1 | 5,081E-02 | 5,006E-02 |
| METRIC TONNE | 1,000E+12 | 1,000E+09 | 1,000E+06 | 3,527E+04 | 2,205E+03 | 1,000E+03 | 1,575E+02 | 6,853E+01 | 1,968E+01 | 1 | 9,852E-01 |
| UK TON | 1,016E+12 | 1,016E+09 | 1,016E+06 | 3,584E+04 | 2,240E+03 | 1,016E+03 | 1,600E+02 | 6,963E+01 | 2,000E+01 | 1,016E+00 | 1 |

# UNITS CONVERSION CHART - PRESSURE

| mm Hg-TORR | kPASCAL - kN/m sq | cm Hg | ft water | inches Hg | lbf / sq in | kgf/sq cm | BAR | ATMOS - PHERE |
|---|---|---|---|---|---|---|---|---|
| 1 | 0,1333 | 0,1 | 4,461E-02 | 3,937E-02 | 1,934E-02 | 1,360E-03 | 1,333E-03 | 1,316E-03 |
| 7,5 | 1 | 0,75 | 0,3346 | 0,2953 | 0,145 | 1,020E-02 | 1,000E-02 | 9,868E-03 |
| 10 | 1,333 | 1 | 0,4461 | 0,3937 | 0,1934 | 1,360E-02 | 1,333E-02 | 1,316E-02 |
| 22,42 | 2,989 | 2,242 | 1 | 0,8826 | 0,4335 | 3,048E-02 | 2,989E-02 | 2,950E-02 |
| 25,4 | 3,387 | 2,54 | 1,133 | 1 | 0,4912 | 3,453E-02 | 3,387E-02 | 3,342E-02 |
| 51,71 | 6,895 | 5,171 | 2,307 | 2,036 | 1 | 7,031E-02 | 6,895E-02 | 6,804E-02 |
| 735,5 | 98,0665 | 73,55 | 32,81 | 28,96 | 14,22 | 1 | 0,9807 | 9,678E-01 |
| 750 | 100 | 75 | 33,46 | 29,53 | 14,5 | 1,02 | 1 | 0,9868 |
| 760 | 101,3 | 76 | 33,9 | 29,92 | 14,7 | 1,033 | 1,013E+00 | 1 |

# UNITS CONVERSION CHART - ENERGY, WORK, HEAT

| ELECTRON VOLT | ERG | JOULE (Nm, Wsec) | FOOT POUND | CALORIE | B.T.U.s | KILO-CALORIE | MEGA JOULE | HORSE POWER-HOUR | kW - HOUR kWh | THERM British Gas |
|---|---|---|---|---|---|---|---|---|---|---|
| 1 | 1,602E-12 | 1,602E-19 | 1,182E-19 | 3,826E-20 | 1,518E-22 | 3,826E-23 | 1,602E-25 | 5,966E-26 | 4,450E-26 | 1,518E-27 |
| 6,242E+11 | 1 | 1,000E-07 | 7,376E-08 | 2,388E-08 | 9,478E-11 | 2,388E-11 | 1,000E-13 | 3,724E-14 | 2,778E-14 | 9,478E-16 |
| 6,242E+18 | 1,000E+07 | 1 | 0,7376 | 2,388E-01 | 9,478E-04 | 2,388E-04 | 1,000E-06 | 3,724E-07 | 2,778E-07 | 9,478E-09 |
| 8,463E+18 | 1,356E+07 | 1,356E+00 | 1 | 0,3238 | 1,285E-03 | 3,238E-04 | 1,356E-06 | 5,049E-07 | 3,766E-07 | 1,285E-08 |
| 2,614E+19 | 41869998,6 | 4,187 | 3,088 | 1 | 3,968E-03 | 1,000E-03 | 4,187E-06 | 1,559E-06 | 1,163E-06 | 3,968E-08 |
| 6,586E+21 | 1,0551E+10 | 1,055E+03 | 7,783E+02 | 2,520E+02 | 1 | 0,2520 | 1,055E-03 | 3,930E-04 | 2,931E-04 | 1,000E-05 |
| 2,614E+22 | 4,187E+10 | 4,187E+03 | 3,088E+03 | 1,000E+03 | 3,968 | 1 | 4,187E-03 | 1,559E-03 | 1,163E-03 | 3,968E-05 |
| 6,242E+24 | 1E+13 | 1,000E+06 | 7,376E+05 | 2,388E+05 | 947,8 | 238,8 | 1 | 0,3724 | 0,2778 | 9,478E-03 |
| 1,676E+25 | 2,685E+13 | 2,685E+06 | 1,981E+06 | 6,413E+05 | 2,545E+03 | 641,3 | 2,685 | 1 | 0,7458 | 2,545E-02 |
| 2,247E+25 | 3,600E+13 | 3,600E+06 | 2,655E+06 | 8,598E+05 | 3,412E+03 | 859,8 | 3,6 | 1,341 | 1 | 3,412E-02 |
| 6,586E+26 | 1,0551E+15 | 1,055E+08 | 7,783E+07 | 2,520E+07 | 1,000E+05 | 2,520E+04 | 105,5 | 39,30 | 29,31 | 1 |

# Tolerance and error calculations

## Resistors in series or parallel

$r_1$ = % **tolerance in $R_1$**
$r_2$ = % **tolerance in $R_2$**   and $r_1 = r_2 = r$

When the resistors have equal % tolerance
then the % tolerance in the total resistance = **r**

## Potential divider

When there is an error in $R_1$ only, then:

the % error in $V_{out}/V_{in} \cong r_1 R_1 / (R_1 + R_2)$

When there is an error in $R_2$ only, then:

the % error in $V_{out}/V_{in} \cong r_2 R_1 / (R_1 + R_2)$

When there is an error in $R_1$ and $R_2$ ; and $r_2 = -r_1 = r$ then:

the worst case % error in $V_{out}/V_{in} = r$

## Inverting Amplifier

$V_{out}/V_{in} = -R_2 / R_1$

$r_1$ = % **error in $R_1$**
$r_2$ = % **error in $R_2$**

The % error in $V_{out}/V_{in}$

(1st aprx) $= r_1 - r_2 - r_1 r_2 /100$

(2nd aprx) $= (r_1 - r_2 - r_1 r_2 /100)(1 + r_2^2 /10^4) + r_2^2 /10^2$

(3rd aprx) $= (r_1 - r_2 - r_1 r_2 /100)(1 + r_2^2 /10^4 + r_2^4 /10^8) + r_2^2 /10^2 + r_2^4 /10^6$

# Bibliography

| | | |
|---|---|---|
| **A Dictionary of Electronics** | S Handel | Penguin Books |
| **Electrical Engineering Circuits** | Hugh Hildreth Skilling | J Wiley & Sons |
| **Electronic Circuits Handbook** | M Tooley | Butterworth-Heinemann |
| **Electronic Designer's Handbook** | T K Hemmingway | Business Publications Ltd |
| **Electronics Pocket Book** | E A Parr | Butterworth-Heinemann |
| **The Art of Electronics** | Horowitz Hill | Cambridge |
| **Thorn Lighting - Technical Handbook** | | Editor: G Williams |

**Technical data books from the following companies:**
**Arcotronics**
**Draloric**
**ERG**
**MFR**
**Neohm**
**Piher**
**Motorola**
**Philips Components**
**Rifa-Evox**
**Roederstein**
**SGS - Thomson**
**Siemens**
**Texas Instruments**
**VTM**
**Welwyn**
**Wima**

# Index